The YARN ANIMAL Book

BY CAROLINE M. STAPLES

Simon and Schuster • New York

Designed by Eve Metz
Manufactured in the United States of America
1   2   3   4   5   6   7   8   9   10

Library of Congress Cataloging in Publication Data

Staples, Caroline M
        The yarn animal book.

        1. Soft toy making.   2. Needlework.   I. Title.
TT174.3.S73   746.4   76-20465
ISBN 0-671-22336-4

ACKNOWLEDGMENTS

Special thanks go to the following people for testing, correcting, improving and redesigning patterns. The book would never have made it without you.

Eli Staples
John Staples
Gay Courter
Phil Courter
Sherri Kuhn
Virginia Staples
Sallie McGrath
Hank McGrath
Kathy Jungjohann
Carol Johnston
V.W.
Marjorie Frazer
Lynn Addison
Lynn Bell
Sandy Dibbin
Debby Dibben
Marge Fowler
Ruth Armstrong
Mrs. Ashbee
Shelley Thibideau
Gwen Thibideau
Ruth Neal

Gloria Hicks
Karen Lozow
Heather Scriven and family
Betty Meeks
Eleanor Hogg
Mr. Hogg
Shelley Connors
Idella Connors
Jean Maxwell
Darla Smith
Joan Topps
Judy Gough
Karen O'Brien
Perry Flonders
Wayne Flonders
Doris Florig
Shirley Genchi
Deborah Pinchback
David Ramsey
Josephine Emrath
Katie de Koster

Contents

7

CHART FINDER

This is a comprehensive list of all the charts that appear throughout the book, to help you find the information you need quickly and easily.

DEAR READER,

Everybody has a favorite stuffed animal tucked away in his memory, or on his pillow. Their charm and appeal are undeniable. Add to that a love of yarns and their many qualities and applications and you have the reason for The Yarn Animal Book.

I started making yarn animals when I was nine years old, as a result of visiting a nursing home. A little lady there made friends with me by teaching me how to make pompoms. From then on she had a regular visitor and everybody I knew got pompoms for Christmas.

The pompoms led to pompom poodles. For years I made poodles and octopi in school colors for the school fair. Back orders kept me busy between fairs. My Latin teacher suggested that the animals belonged in a book. Personally, I was glad to graduate and get away from the manufacturing-at-home business.

When my friends started having babies I was caught again. Each baby got a mobile with pompom birds, cats, fish, bears and octopi; each baby, that is, until my own arrived. He got three pieces of colored paper dangling from string. By then I was deep into the book. The idea was that Eli would have the most wonderful stuffed animals in the world. Instead he spent his early months playing with the rejects—the giraffe who couldn't stand up, the half-stuffed Scottie, the two-legged octopus, the hippo who stood on his nose because it weighed more than his body, and assorted beaks, tails and legs that didn't belong to anyone in particular.

I'd read enough articles on two-year-olds to realize that the book was a now or never proposition. Even with the help of John, Nip and Carol there looked like no end in sight. We had just moved to a farm outside of Burks Falls, Ontario, and I didn't know anybody. So I placed an ad in the Almaguin News asking for volunteers of all ages, sexes, abilities and interests. To my surprise, people started to call. We share a seven-party line so our unfortunate neighbors had to put up with all the ringing. (Special thanks to them for their patience.) There were more volunteers than animals at first. I was so excited about all the help that I didn't want to turn anyone away, so I kept adding new animal patterns and the book got bigger and bigger.

The volunteers tested, corrected, improved, redesigned and rewrote all the patterns. It turned out to be an ideal way for a newcomer to make friends and learn the back roads. When I went to pick up animals there was often something extra—a jar of jam, a bunch of dill, brown eggs, cucumbers. And over a cup of tea I would hear each animal's own story. Lucy Llama's tail had been changed because Mrs. Hogg had visited the llamas at the Toronto zoo. Sandy's knit elephant and knit owl won first and second place at the Burks Falls Fair. Ruth burned her hand making lollipops for her little brother so her knit turtle didn't make it to the fair. The orangutan's rya stitch bothered Jean Maxwell's arthritis. Scottie didn't get hurt when he and Heather fell down the cellar stairs together. V.W. managed to add another animal to the menagerie every week and her designer's instinct was invaluable. And I can't leave out Muriel. One day I followed a herd of cows to the end of a dirt road. The dust settled and there, in the middle of nowhere, was Muriel's amazing yarn shop. It was unbelievable. She had everything I needed, including a husband who played with Eli while she and I discussed yarns.

The stories go on and on. Somehow the animals, manuscript and illustrations arrived at the office of my ever-patient editor, Julie Houston, who will pass them on to you.

My special hope is that you will enjoy making these animals as much as I have.

With love and best wishes,

Carrie Staples

Carrie Staples

P. S. Thank you again, John and Julie, for all your patience.

I
GENERAL INFORMATION

All About Yarn

Yarn is made from a combination of many fine, hair-like fibers—natural, man-made or a combination of both—that are spun together to give the yarn body and strength.

In the past, yarns were made from only one type of fiber, such as wool or cotton. Now there are many blended yarns made by twisting two or more different kinds of fibers together. Using different kinds of fibers in the same yarn gives the new yarn special qualities from each. Natural fibers include animal fibers, such as wool and angora, and vegetable fibers, such as cotton, linen and jute. Among the man-made fibers normally used in hand-knitting are acrylics, polyesters and blends. Polyesters are made from coal, air, water and petroleum. Acrylic yarns are a type of plastic fiber.

Ply is the term used to describe how many strands are twisted together to make the yarn. For example, if three strands are twisted together, it is called 3-ply yarn. However, a 6-ply yarn isn't necessarily heavier than a 3-ply yarn. The thickness of the separate strands varies. If the strands in a 3-ply yarn are twice as thick as those in a 6-ply yarn, both yarns will be the same weight. The 3-ply yarn would tend to be fluffier and have more give. The 6-ply yarn would probably wear better, assuming that the quality of the yarns was similar, and it would be less pliable.

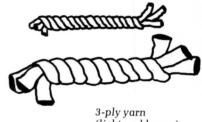

*3-ply yarn
(light and heavy)*

• WOOL VERSUS SYNTHETICS

Wool makes a strong, bouncy, resilient, long-wearing yarn. It comes in a wide range of colors and is sold everywhere. Wool has traditionally been considered "better" than synthetics, but that opinion is gradually changing as synthetics improve and come closer to matching the qualities of wool, or provide special quali-

15

ties which wool doesn't have. Nowadays, wool is expected to equal synthetic yarns in the ability to withstand machine-washing. When buying wool yarns, it is wise to check labels to see that the product is preshrunk, moth-proofed and machine-washable. These are important qualities for a child's toy.

Common synthetic yarns you might work with are polyesters, acrylics, nylon and Orlon. Some bulky acrylic and polyester craft yarns and rug yarns come in very bright colors which have a slight sheen. Sometimes they are stiff and don't work up as easily as other types of yarns, but they stand up well to wear and they wash easily. Loose tension will cause stretching in synthetics, especially bulky yarns. You may find that the glue you normally use to attach felt features to the animals doesn't stick to some acrylic and polyester yarns. Sew the pieces of felt instead.

Some synthetics tend to "pill," a term describing small balls of fiber which appear on the surface of a synthetic piece after a short period of wear. Pilling is caused by short fibers in the yarn (often found in cheaper yarns, since long fibers are more expensive). Orlon resists pilling, while nylon tends to pill. Other polyester and acrylic yarns are soft and easy to work with. The discussion of these problems does not mean that you should avoid these yarns— they are constantly improving, and usually their advantages outweigh any problems.

Regardless of your preferences, invest wisely in the yarn that you buy. Cheaper yarns in both wool and man-made fibers won't wear as well as better quality yarns of any type. Cheaper yarns are usually made of short fibers which don't hold up as well as long fibers.

• ESTIMATING HOW MUCH YARN TO BUY

Buy enough yarn for a project *all at once*. Always buy enough yarn of the same dye lot (check the dye lot number on the label) to complete the project. Yarns dyed in one batch may be of a noticeably different color than yarns dyed in another batch, even though both have the same color name on the label. Sometimes the difference is unnoticed until you have worked the two dye lots together, and then you may not be able to find the same dye lot again.

When figuring length of yarn, remember that a 4-ounce skein of bulky yarn will be shorter than a 4-ounce skein of knitting worsted. Knitting worsted has about 75 yards per ounce. Double knitting yarn has about 60 yards per ounce. Sport yarns run about 115 yards per ounce. Judging weights of yarn is difficult because each yarn manufacturer uses his own terminology.

To estimate how much yarn to buy, work a sample square with the weight of yarn you plan to use. To estimate accurately, the swatch should be:

2″ to 3″ square for needlepoint

3″ to 4″ square for knitting and crocheting

3″ to 4″ square for rya or hooking

Measure how many yards of yarn you use as you make the swatch. Figure the number of square inches of each color needed and multiply each by the number of yards of yarn used in a square inch of the sample (or the number of square inches made or covered by a yard of yarn). To find out how many packages of yarn to buy, divide the number of yards needed by the number of yards in a package. Yarn is packaged and sold in many shapes and weights:

Fold-over skeins (looped skeins that must be wound into balls)

Pull-out skeins (wound skeins that are pulled from the center)

Cones

Hanks

Pre-cut strands

By ounces, pounds, grams, etc.

If you are still not sure about how much you'll need, ask someone in your yarn store for help. It's better to buy more yarn than you think you'll need. Many yarn shops will take back unopened skeins of yarn, probably because it is so hard to figure yarn yardage accurately.

• CHOOSING YARNS

Each project in this book has an indication of the yarn type and weight. But these are only suggestions. You can use anything that meets the requirements of the project. If the yarn is going to be pulled through a canvas for needlepoint, crewel or rya, it shouldn't stretch, shred or pill. If the yarn you want to use in a needlepoint or bargello project doesn't cover the canvas completely, use a doubled strand. If you want to use a yarn that is too heavy to go through the canvas or fabric, tack it down with a couching stitch.

If you want to use a lighter weight yarn than is called for in a knit or crochet project, you have two alternatives. You can knit or crochet with the yarn doubled or you can use a single strand and end up with a project smaller than the original. Remember to use smaller needles or hooks if you are working with lighter yarn.

17

Start pull-out skein here.

2 strands sport yarn = 1 strand knitting worsted
2 strands knitting worsted = 1 strand bulky or craft yarn
1 knitting worsted + 1 bulky = 1 strand rug yarn

A wonderfully fuzzy effect is created when you combine a strand of mohair yarn with a strand of knitting worsted. Experiment with any of the new, textured yarns. How about using jute, hardware string, macrame cord, soutache braid, ribbon, etc., in place of or combined with yarn?

Experiment! Everybody loves a stuffed animal, so no matter what you do, your animal will find a home. The worst (or is it the best?) thing people will say is that your animal is unusual. And from my point of view, that's great!

• WASHING YARNS

Check for the manufacturer's washing instructions, which often come on the yarn, or ask the salesperson. Many of the man-made yarns and wools are machine-washable. If there are no instructions, the safest thing to do is to wash the item in cold or lukewarm water and mild soap. Wash gently and quickly. Soak for stubborn stains. Do not rub! Rinse thoroughly. Squeeze excess water out gently and roll or wrap in a turkish towel. If you're working with flat pieces, stretch them into the correct shapes and let dry in the air away from sunlight. If it's a completed and stuffed yarn animal, follow same drying instructions, turning the animal every so often. Follow the same instructions for cotton yarns but wash in hot water. If you decide to have the item dry-cleaned, tell the cleaners what kind of yarn or yarns were used.

Choosing Colors

Color combinations are suggested for projects in this book. Often I used a particular color because that was what was available when I decided to work on the project. If you have another color idea, try it. Maybe you want to match a decorating color scheme or blend school colors. Experiment. Colors can be mixed in all kinds of unusual ways. Purple, orange and pink look great together. Gold, magenta, green and black can look very lively. People used to think that blue and brown didn't "go together," but they can actually look very nice—it just depends on the shades selected.

The color wheel can help you get started. The following color schemes are based on the color wheel.

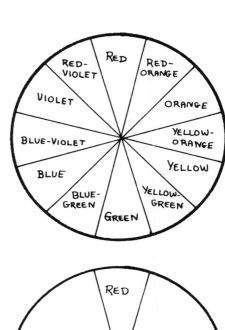

COMPLEMENTARY COLORS: Complete contrast, like red and green. They are on opposite sides of the color wheel.

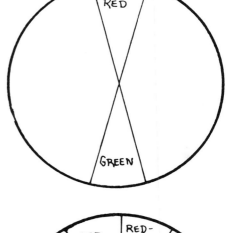

ANALOGOUS COLORS: Similar colors, like red and red-orange. They are harmonious and are found right next to each other on the color wheel.

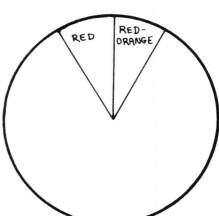

19

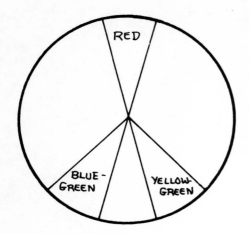

SPLIT COMPLEMENTARY COLORS: A three-color scheme with two related colors and one strong contrast, like blue-green and yellow-green plus red.

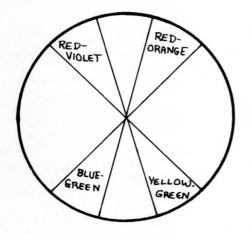

DOUBLE SPLIT COMPLEMENTARY: A four-color scheme—two related sets of complementary colors.

You can also try these color schemes without using a color wheel:

MONOCHROMATIC COLOR SCHEME: Consists of colors in the same color family like light blue, medium blue and navy blue. This makes a very sophisticated combination.

VARIEGATED COLORS: Buy variegated, ombré or tweed yarns that have color variation and coordination built in. Or use two different shades of 2-ply yarn where 4-ply yarn is called for to get a different, sort of tweedy effect.

NEUTRAL COLORS: Black, white, grays, off-white, beiges.

WARM COLORS: Red, red-orange, yellow, yellow-orange and yellow-green.

COOL COLORS: Blue, blue-green, green, violet.

Other Materials and Technical Suggestions

• STUFFINGS

COTTON BATTING: Gets used up fast. Tends to mat when washed. Medium priced.

POLYESTER FIBERFILL (POLYFILL): Like the stuff used for quilting. It's my favorite since it doesn't stick to yarn, doesn't come through holes, washes well and dries quickly. Very easy to work with. Tends to be expensive.

NYLON NETTING: Good for stuffing small animals. Easy to work with. Washes well, dries quickly. A little goes a long way so it is inexpensive. Use it only in lightweight animals.

FOAM CHIPS: Inexpensive. Makes nice, squishy animals. Doesn't wear as well as others. My main objection to it is that the chips stick to the yarn and are impossible to brush off completely. Also the chips tend to come through holes in the knitting, crocheting or whatever.

NYLON STOCKINGS: Excellent if you have a lot of them.

RAGS: Good. They make the animal heavy, which may be what you want for certain animals. Just make sure they're colorfast.

STUFFING COMBINATIONS: In a large and/or tall animal like the llama, it is a good idea to stuff the lower half of the animal with something heavy like rags. Then stuff the upper half, including the long neck and head, with something light like polyfill. That way the animal is sturdy, well-balanced and yet not top-heavy.

• GLUES

When working with mesh canvas and loose-weave materials, glues are indispensable. Use them around the outside of patterns on loose-weave materials so they don't fray around the edges. Use them around mesh patterns so the mesh doesn't come apart. There are special fabric glues like Jiffy Sew and Magic Mender. Or you can use white glues (which I do) like Sobo and Elmer's.

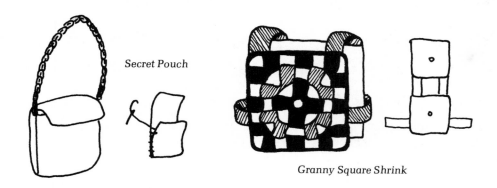

Secret Pouch

Granny Square Shrink

• YARN CLOTHES FOR THE ANIMALS

If you want to make clothes for your animal, it is easy to crochet up some simple things. Put granny squares together to make vests and bags. Follow the instructions for the turtle's hat for a nice cap. Work to whatever size will fit your animal.

If you can't crochet, knit simple squares and put them together just like the granny squares.

There are instructions for a fabric beret included with the hooked Scottie. It would look nice on other animals, too.

• INTERCHANGEABLE TECHNIQUES

You may be surprised to know that one technique can sometimes be substituted for another—for example, knitting for crochet, and needlepoint for crewel. In the first case, it is simply a matter of figuring the gauge of your work, and the size of the piece you want to make. Specific interchangeable projects appear on p. 205 of the Crochet section, and you may want to work out other substitutions for yourself. In interchanging needlepoint and crewel, it is a simple matter of making sure that the different size of your embroidery stitches will not affect the total effect of the finished product.

Suggested Projects for Young People to Make

Here is a list of animals which can be made by people under nine years of age (or by anyone looking for something extra-easy): Mini-Monster Friend; woolly octopus; crewel pig; crewel fish; rya hedgehog; knit elephant, owl, cat, or turtle; any-animal puppet; Mr. Big-Mouth Puppet.

These animals, in addition to those above, can be made by people under twelve years of age: all woolly animals; rya broom-stick bear or pony; rya lion; crewel bird; crewel hippo; needle-point snail; needlepoint cat; all knit animals; crocheted kiwi; Corky the Bookworm; crocheted dragonfly, butterfly, or piggy bag.

II

WOOLLY
ANIMALS

Woolly animals have a special cuddle quality. It's like wiggling your toes in a deep pile carpet. They are also the easiest toys to make.

Start a child out making a Mini-Monster Friend, p. 37. Or make one yourself in minutes. there is no end to the way the eight yarn techniques illustrated here can be put together. Try one of these animal designs or create your own.

Note: The term "yarn" does not refer to any specific type of yarn in this section. The patterns were worked out using knitting-worsted weight yarn but any kind of yarn can be substituted. To make a pattern go faster, use a bulky yarn. For extra-soft animals, use baby yarn. For variety, include a strand of textured, nubby or fuzzy yarn. Try using several different strands at once. Experiment with variegated, ombré and tweed yarns. Anything goes.

General Directions

• POMPOMS

How to make pompoms 2″ in diameter or larger.

MATERIALS
    Yarn (see note, p. 27)
    Thin cardboard
    Scissors
    Ruler
    Pencil
    Compass (or a round object that is close to the size of the pompom you want to make)
    Paper clip (or needle, piece of wire, pipe cleaner or other object suitable for threading yarn)
    Buttonhole thread (optional, holds pompoms together very well)

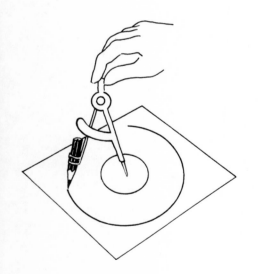

Draw two donuts on the cardboard as shown. If the finished pompom is to be 2″ in diameter, make the outside diameter of the donut 2″. The size of the donut hole determines how dense the pompom will be. The larger the center hole, the thicker the pompom will be.

AVERAGE POMPOM PROPORTIONS

Outside diameter	Inside diameter
2″	¾″
3″	1″
4″	1½″
5″	2″

Thread a paper clip with 3 strands of yarn.

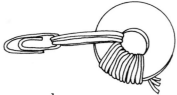

Put the cardboard donuts together and wrap the yarn around them, working through the center hole.

When all the yarn has been wrapped around, remove the paper clip. Re-thread it and continue wrapping yarn, following the same procedure, until it is difficult to slip the paper clip through the center of the donut hole. There is no need to tie any ends together. Just cover the loose ends as you wrap the next layer of yarn around.

Clip yarn around the outside edges of the circle until you can slip the scissors between the cardboard circles. Cut all the strands holding the two circles together.

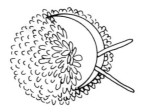

Wrap a strand of yarn or buttonhole thread down between the cardboard donuts. Wind it around the yarn several times and tie tightly.

Cut the cardboard donuts to the center and remove them carefully. They can be repaired with tape and used again.

Fluff out the pompom and trim it to a rounded shape.

29

Quick Projects

Add a felt face and feet and hang the pompom from a cord to amuse a baby or to decorate a Christmas tree.

Or add a felt face and pipe-cleaner legs covered in felt to make a mini-monster.

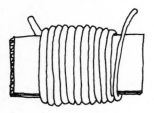

• HOW TO MAKE SMALL POMPOMS

MATERIALS
    Yarn (see note, p. 27)
    Cardboard
    Scissors
    Ruler
    Pencil
    Buttonhole thread (optional, see "Pompoms")

To make one small pompom, measure and cut a piece of cardboard 1½" by 3". Wrap yarn around the 1½" width about 40 times.

Cut the yarn across both ends of the cardboard. Pile the yarn neatly and tie the pile tightly at the middle. Leave long yarn ends for attaching the pompom. Trim the rest to a neat ball about 1" in diameter.

30

· HOW TO MAKE 10 SMALL POMPOMS ALL AT ONCE

MATERIALS
    Yarn (see note, p. 27)
    Cardboard
    Scissors
    Ruler
    Pencil
    Buttonhole thread (optional, see "Pompoms")

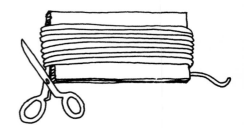

Wind yarn 100 times around a piece of cardboard 12″ long. Clip the strands at one end and lay the yarn strands out in a long, neat pile.

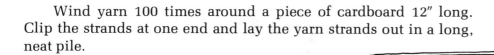

Wrap a piece of yarn around the strands 1″ from one end and tie off tightly. Continue to tie the yarn pile at 2″ intervals until you reach the other end. There should be a total of 10 ties (ties take up extra yarn length resulting in 10 pompoms instead of 12).

Cut the tied-off pile into bunches halfway between each tie.

Fluff each bunch into a pompom and trim to a round shape. There should be 10 pompoms.

• MINI-POMPOMS

These pompoms are ½″ inch or smaller in diameter.

MATERIALS
      Yarn (see note, p. 27)
      Scissors
      Pencil

      Lay a piece of yarn or buttonhole thread along a pencil. If you are going to tie the mini-pompom onto an animal, this piece of yarn should be the same color as the animal.
      Wrap a second piece of yarn around the pencil and yarn strip 40 times, more if you want a fuller pompom. The second piece of yarn very often will be a contrasting color to the first.
      Slip the yarn wrapping off the pencil. Take ends A and B and tie, pulling tightly to gather loops.

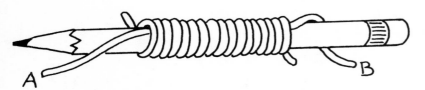

Clip the loops and trim the pompom.

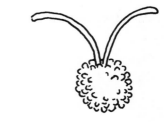

Quick Projects

MAGNET ANIMALS: Try making tiny animals and creatures by tieing or sewing mini-pompoms together. Glue on felt features. Then sew or glue a small magnet or large safety pin to the back of the animal so you can stick it to your refrigerator door or pin it to your hat. Or how about dangling the little creature from a suction cup or a spring?

32

• BRAIDS

MATERIALS

    Yarn (see note, p. 27)
    Cardboard
    Scissors
    Ruler
    Pencil

Cut out a piece of cardboard which is 3 times as long as the finished braid should be. Wrap yarn around the cardboard 12 times. Clip the yarn at one end of the cardboard.

    Tie the yarn tightly at the other end.
    Divide the yarn into 3 equal bunches (8 strands per bunch) and braid.

Note: For fatter braids, wind more yarn around the cardboard.

• TASSELS

MATERIALS

    Yarn (see note, p. 27)
    Cardboard
    Scissors
    Ruler
    Pencil

Cut a piece of cardboard 2″ wide and as long as the tassel is supposed to be. Wrap yarn around the length of the cardboard 20 times. Clip the yarn at one end of the cardboard.

Lay the yarn out in a neat pile and tie it tightly around the middle. Leave these tie ends long to attach tassel.

Fold the yarn in half at the tie. Wrap a strand of yarn tightly around the yarn about 1″ below the top and tie it off, leaving ends the length of the tassel. Trim the bottom of the tassel.

Note: For fatter tassels, wind more yarn around the cardboard or use thicker yarn.

• LOOPS

MATERIALS
    Yarn (see note, p. 27)
    Cardboard
    Scissors
    Ruler
    Pencil

Cut a piece of cardboard to size given in project directions, usually 2½″ to 4″ long by 2″ wide. Wrap yarn around the length of the cardboard 13 times. Tie the two yarn ends together.

Slip the yarn off the cardboard. Tie the two ends tightly around the middle of the yarn to make a loop.

• WOOLLY STRIPS

Instead of stringing pompoms together, fluffy bodies, legs, heads and tails can also be made this way. They take longer to make but hold up better under rough usage.

MATERIALS

Yarn: The directions below apply to knitting worsted. If you use bulky yarn the strip will be fuller and fatter. You need about ⅔ as many wraps of yarn. For example, a cardboard strip 1¾" wide wrapped with knitting worsted will give you a 1¾" wide woolly strip. The same 1¾" cardboard will give you a 2¼" strip if you substitute craft yarn.

    Cardboard, heavy weight or doubled
    Ruler
    Pencil
    Scissors
    Pipe cleaner(s) or stiff white cotton cord
    Needle and strong thread

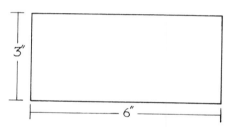

To make a fat strip, like a body section, cut a rectangle of cardboard as long and as wide as the woolly strip you want to make. The following illustrations demonstrate how to make a strip 3" by 6".

Draw lines dividing the 3" side into thirds.

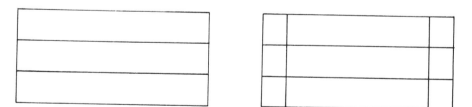

Draw lines across the 6" length, ¾" in from each end.
Cut out the center section.
Wrap yarn around the cardboard working neatly back and forth from one end of the cardboard to the other—approximately 300 times.

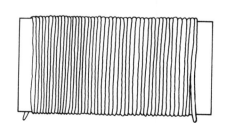

Note: You can save time by wrapping 2 or 3 strands of yarn around the cardboard at once.

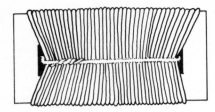

Slip pipe cleaner around the yarn, inside the frame, and twist the ends together. (If necessary, use two pipe cleaners—twist ends together to make one long one.) Do not wrap the pipe cleaners around the yarn too tightly.

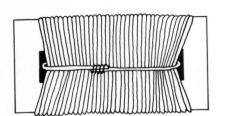

Note: If you want to use cord or string instead of pipecleaners, follow the same steps, tying the ends of the string in a square knot. Tie the knot where it will join another part of the animal, in the middle of a leg strip, and at the end of a body strip. That way the string tails can be used to tie the parts together. Don't use cord any heavier than #30 cable cotton or the cord will show.

Sew the pipe cleaners (or cord) together by passing the needle and thread *through* the yarn and *around* the pipe cleaners from back to front to back, etc., so that the yarn and pipe cleaners are securely joined from one end of the strip to the other.

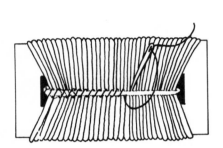

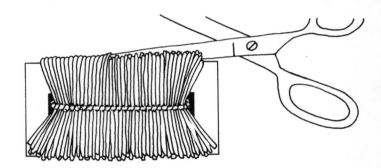

Clip the yarn along both edges and remove the woolly strip. Don't trim it until after the animal has been put together.

To Make Thin Strips: For parts like legs and tails, cut the cardboard strip 2″ longer than the length you want and then follow the same directions as for fat strips. Wrap yarn around leg strips 350 times. For thin tail strips (for example, kitten's tail), wrap 200 times.

Quick Project

Put a felt face on the fat woolly strip and you have a Woolly Bear Caterpillar. He'll look even more real if you wind the yarn in alternating stripes of color.

The Projects

• MINI-MONSTER FRIEND

This is the fastest and easiest gift to make in the whole book. And it's extra loveable to both tots and teens. David made a mini-monster one morning when he had a cold and couldn't go to kindergarten. He guarantees that it will take no more than a half hour from start to finish.

MATERIALS

    2 oz. yarn (2 colors work well)
    Piece of cardboard, 5″ by about 4″
    Scissors
    Bits of felt
    White glue
    Buttonhole thread (optional)

If you use two colors, wind both strands of yarn together around the 5″ length of cardboard 150 times. (If you use one color, wrap it around the cardboard 300 times.)

Slip a piece of yarn through between the cardboard and the yarn and tie it tightly around the yarn at one end. Clip the yarn at the other end.

Tie the yarn around the middle again with a doubled strand of yarn or buttonhole thread to make it extra secure.

Trim the long, shaggy ends along the bottom neatly.

Make one small pompom according to the instructions at the beginning of this section (p. 30). It will be the nose. It can be made from one of the colors you are using or from a different, contrasting color. Tie the nose on around 15 strands of yarn in the bunch so that it hangs in an interesting position.

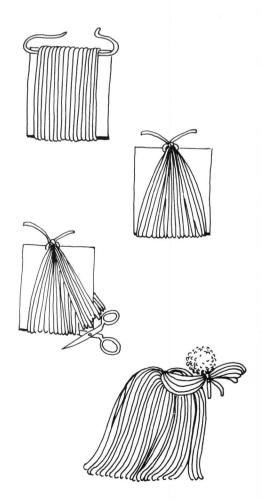

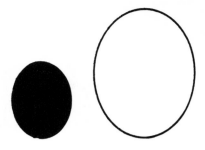

Make 2 eyes by tracing the following patterns and cutting them out of felt. Or design your own. Glue the eyes on beside the nose.

Note: A group of mini-monsters makes an excellent mobile.

• CUDDLY CATERPILLAR

The following instructions are for making a fat, 20″-long caterpillar. If you want to make a smaller caterpillar, just make smaller pompoms and follow the same directions for putting them together. If you want a longer caterpillar, make more pompoms. Adjust eye patterns accordingly.

MATERIALS
   8 oz. blue yarn
   8 oz. green yarn
   (Or use any colors you like and as many different colors as you want.)
   Cardboard
   Bits of felt
   Scissors
   White glue
   Ruler
   Compass
   Scotch tape
   String
   Paper clip

Make the parts for the caterpillar by following the instructions for pompoms (p. 28) and small pompoms (p. 30) at the beginning of this section. The parts needed are:

Pompoms: Make 3 green pompoms and 3 blue pompoms, all on 5″ diameter cardboard donuts with 2″ diameter center holes.

Small pompoms: Make 1 small blue pompom, 1″ in diameter.

To assemble, string the pompoms through their centers with a doubled piece of string "threaded" on the paper clip, alternating colors. Make sure the string passes through the center tie in each pompom. Tie the string tightly so the pompoms are pulled close together.

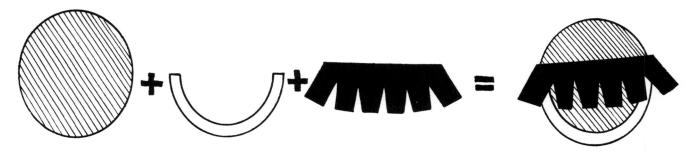

Make 2 droopy eyes by tracing the following patterns and cutting them out of felt.

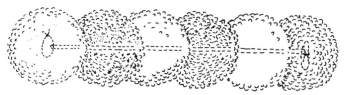

Tie the small blue pompom around the head of the caterpillar to make his nose. Glue the eyes on either side of the nose.

To make a mouth, cut a piece of felt as indicated. Separate the yarn at a good spot for a mouth and glue the felt piece in.

To make hair, wrap blue yarn around a 4″-wide piece of cardboard 40 times. Clip the yarn at one end and tie it together in the middle, leaving long ends on the ties. Tie the "hair" around the head tightly so that it sticks out at the top of the head.

• PANDA BEAR

Add a red bow and sit him on top of a special Christmas present or hang him from your tree. He's easy to make and he'll win every heart. Put him together with string instead of pipe cleaners for little children.

MATERIALS
    1½ oz. white yarn
    ½ oz. black yarn
    Scraps of black and white felt
    Cardboard
    Compass
    Scissors
    Pencil
    White glue
    Pipe cleaners or string

Make the parts for the panda by following the instructions at the beginning of this section. The parts needed are:
    Pompoms: Make one 3″ white pompom and one 2½″ white pompom.
    Small pompoms: Make 8 small black pompoms.

To assemble, trim 5 of the small black pompoms so that they are oblong, rather than round, for use as paws and tail.
    Trim the remaining 3 black pompoms so that they are 1″ in diameter and round, for ears and nose.

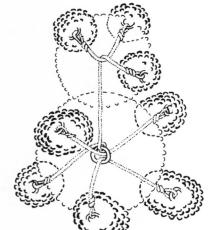

String all the parts of the panda together with pipe cleaners or string, as shown.

Make eyes by tracing the following patterns and cutting them out of felt.

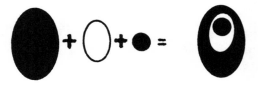

Glue the eyes on and the panda is complete.

• POMPOM POODLE PUP

I broke my leg skiing on the first day of spring vacation when I was about fourteen. The result was that I spent a week in the hospital making poodles for all the doctors and nurses. These perky little dogs are lots of fun for kids to make because you can finish one in about an hour. Make the pompoms out of two colors of yarn for a special effect.

MATERIALS
    1 oz. yellow yarn
    1 oz. white yarn
    6 pipe cleaners
    Bits of felt
    Scissors
    White glue
    Ruler
    Piece of cardboard, 12″ x 6″

Make the parts for the pompom poodle by following the instructions at the beginning of this section. The parts needed are:
    Small pompoms: Make 20 small pompoms by following the instructions on how to make 10 small pompoms twice. Wind the yellow and white yarns around the cardboard together 50 times to make multicolored pompoms. Cut the pompoms apart but don't trim them until the animal has been put together.
    Tassels: Make 2 tassels. Wind yellow and white yarns around the 6″ width of the cardboard 4 times.

To assemble, twist the ends of two pipe cleaners together so they won't pull apart. Do the same with the other two pairs of pipe cleaners.

String 8 pompoms on one of the lengthened pipe cleaners. String 6 pompoms on each of the other lengthened pipe cleaners. Clip the pipe cleaners 1″ beyond the last pompom at each end. Fold the ends back on themselves and twist well to lock the pompoms on. Then slide the pompoms over the twisted parts.

Bend each of the two sets of pipe cleaners with 6 pompoms in half to make legs. Twist 1 set of legs around the 8-pompom strip between the fourth and fifth pompoms. Twist the other set of legs between the sixth and seventh pompoms, counting from the same end.

Bend the head and tail into shape.

Clip the long ends off and give the pup a poodle cut by trimming as indicated.

Tie the tassels onto the poodle behind the second pompom so that they stick out at the sides of the pup's head for ears.

Make a face by gluing bits of felt on for eyes, nose and tongue.

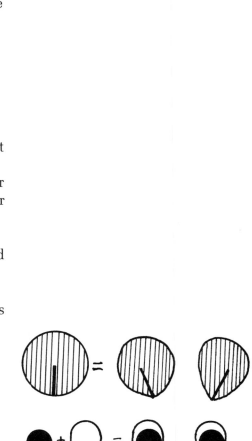

• SQUEEZABLE SQUIRREL

This squirrel looks real if you make him out of natural brown or gray yarn. The special thing about this little fellow is that he's guaranteed to cheer you up.

MATERIALS
> 2½ oz. yarn
> Thin cardboard
> Scissors
> Ruler
> Pencil
> Compass (or a round object that is close to the size of the pompom you want to make)
> 2 pipe cleaners
> Bits of felt
> White glue
> Scotch tape
> Paper clip or large needle

Make the parts for the squirrel by following the instructions at the beginning of this section. The parts needed are:
> Pompoms: Make 1 pompom on a 3″ donut with a 1″ center hole. Then make 2 pompoms on a 2″ donut with a ½″ center hole.
> Small pompoms: Make 2 small pompoms 1″ in diameter.
> Loops: Make 20 loops on a 2½″ length of cardboard. Braid tightly.
> Braids: Make 2 braids on a 6″ length of cardboard.
> Pipe cleaners: Hook the pipe cleaners together with the ends twisted back on themselves.

To assemble, trim one 2″ pompom to a point on one side to make the squirrel's face.

Attach head to one end of the pipe cleaners and twist the end of the pipe cleaner back around itself tightly. Cut eyes, nose, tongue and ears out of felt and glue them on.

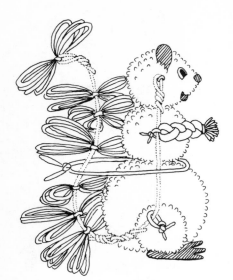

String the other 2″ and then the 3″ pompom onto the pipe cleaners.

Tie the braids onto the middle pompom to make arms.

Make 2

Tie the two 1″ pompoms on either side of the 3″ pompom to make legs. Cut out of felt and glue to the bottoms of the legs.

String the loops onto the pipe cleaner end to make a tail. Slide the loops down tightly and twist the end of the pipe cleaner back around itself.

Tie the tail and the body together around the middle with a piece of yarn so the tail doesn't flop over. The squirrel is complete.

Note: If you don't want to use pipe cleaners, the squirrel can be threaded together with heavy string. Tie the tail to the body in several places so it won't flop too much.

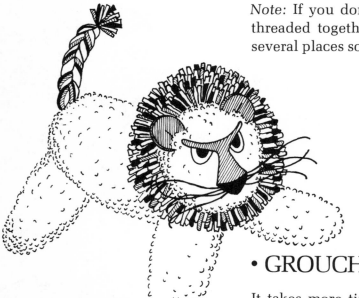

• GROUCHY LION

It takes more time to make woolly strips than pompoms but because they are sewn together, they can't be pulled apart. That's a very important quality for the pre-school set who love to stick their fingers into deep, cuddly fur.

MATERIALS

    3 oz. orange yarn
    Scraps of yellow and orange rug yarn (optional)
    Bits of black, white and orange felt
    8 pipe cleaners

Cardboard
Ruler
Compass
Scissors
Pencil
Needle and heavy thread
Black buttonhole thread
White glue

Make the parts for the lion by following the instructions at the beginning of this section. The parts needed are:

Woolly strips: Make 1 orange woolly strip on a 6″ x 2¼″ piece of cardboard for the body.

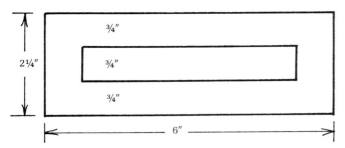

2¼″

¾″

¾″

¾″

6″

Drawn to ½ scale.

Make 2 orange woolly strips on a 9½″ x 1⅛″ piece of cardboard for legs.

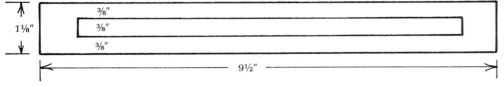

1⅛″

⅜″

⅜″

⅜″

9½″

Drawn to ½ scale.

Pompoms: Make 1 orange pompom on 3½″ cardboard rings with 1¼″ inside holes. If you have scraps of orange and/or yellow rug yarn, mix them with the regular yarn on half of the ring.

Clip the pompom so the regular yarn side of the ball is smaller than the half with rug yarn, which will be the lion's mane.

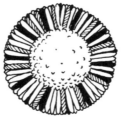

Regular yarn

Mixture of rug yarn
and regular yarn

FRONT VIEW

SIDE VIEW

45

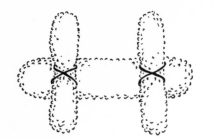

Braids: Make 1 tight braid, 4″ long. If you make it with rug yarn, use 6 wraps. If you make it with regular yarn, use 12 wraps.

To assemble, sew the middle of each leg section securely to the body section, 1″ from each end.

Tie the head to one end of the body and the tail to the other. Trim the lion if he needs it.

Make face and ears by tracing the following patterns. Cut them out of felt and glue them to the head. Make whiskers out of black buttonhole thread, as shown.

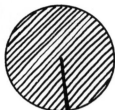

WHITE

ORANGE

BLACK

Glue whiskers behind nose.

Tuck one side behind and glue.

• ST. BERNARD PUP

This little fellow wasn't going to be included but he snuck into the picture. So here he is with brief instructions. He works especially well in natural color bulky wool yarn.

MATERIALS
    3 oz. dark, bulky wool yarn or craft yarn
    1½ oz. light, bulky wool yarn or craft yarn
    Pipecleaners or string

Felt scraps
Cardboard
Buttonhole thread
See "Grouchy Lion" for rest of supplies

Make the parts for the puppy by following the instructions at the beginning of this section. The parts needed are:

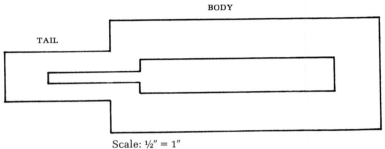

BODY

TAIL

Scale: ½″ = 1″

HEAD
1¾″ x 5″ woolly strip.

BODY AND TAIL
See diagram for woolly strip measurements.

WINDING INSTRUCTIONS

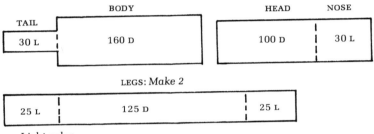

TAIL	BODY		HEAD	NOSE
30 L	160 D		100 D	30 L

LEGS: *Make 2*

25 L	125 D	25 L

L—*Light color*
D—*Dark color*

LEGS
Two 9½″ x 1¼″ woolly strips.

Note: See Illustration. It shows how many times to wind yarn around each area of the woolly strips.

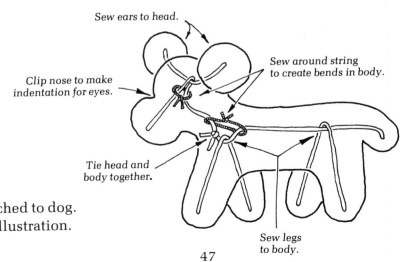

Sew ears to head.

Clip nose to make indentation for eyes.

Sew around string to create bends in body.

Tie head and body together.

Sew legs to body.

EARS
2 small pompoms.

Note: Don't trim until they are attached to dog.
Put the puppy together following Illustration.

47

• LOOPY LAMB

There's something about the loopy lamb that makes everybody want one. I knew an associate professor in an engineering department who had two sitting on his bookcase. So gather the materials and make one while you watch your favorite TV programs. The first lamb will be finished in an evening or two and then you'll be ready to start on the second one.

MATERIALS
> 8 oz. yarn
> Cardboard strip, 4″ x 2″
> Coat hanger—the thinner the wire, the better
> Scissors
> Pliers (helpful but not necessary)
> Heavy duty tape (adhesive tape, electrician's tape, adhesive bandage)
> Scraps of black yarn
> Pencil

Make the parts for the loopy lamb by following the instructions at the beginning of this section. The parts needed are:
> Loops: As many as you can make out of 8 oz. of yarn, saving a little to make 2 tassels. Make the loops on the 4″ length of the cardboard.
> Mini-Pompom: Make 1 black mini-pompom.
> Tassels: Make 2 tassels on the 4″ length of the cardboard. Wrap them 25 times each.

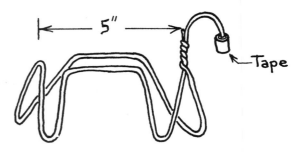

To assemble, bend the coat hanger as shown, using pliers if you have them. Wrap a piece of tape around the hook end of the hanger.

Tie the yarn loops around the coat hanger in alternating directions. Pack them in tightly.

Tie on tassels for ears.

Tie on the mini-pompom for a nose.

Make eye lashes by looping bits of black yarn around a couple of loops where you want the eyes to be, as shown. Trim the lashes.

• OCTOPUS

Make the two-color octopus described below in your school colors and you'll have a sure seller at the school fair. This octopus is solid yarn instead of having stuffing or a ball inside his head. Because of that, if you braid the legs tightly the shorter octopi will stand up by themselves.

MATERIALS
    3 oz. yarn
    Piece of cardboard, 12″ x about 4″
    Scissors
    Bits of felt
    White glue

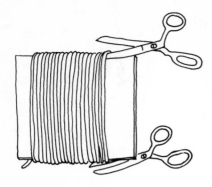

Wrap yarn around the 12″ length of cardboard 192 times. Clip the yarn at the top and bottom of the cardboard.

Pile the cut yarn together. Tie the bundle tightly 1½″ from the top. Tie it again 3½″ below the first tie. This makes the head.

Braid the rest of yarn into 8 legs. Use 48 strands per leg if you want to count, but an approximation works just as well. Braid legs tightly. Tie each braid off securely and trim any long ends.

Cut eyes, nose and mouth out of felt and glue the features onto the head.

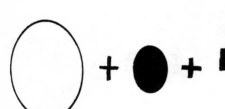

Push the yarn at the top of the head down and trim it so that it looks like hair.

TRY DIFFERENT FACES

Variations

TWO-COLOR, STRIPED OCTOPUS: Use 1½ ounces of each color. Wrap Color A around the cardboard 96 times. Divide the cut yarn into 4 separate piles. Do the same with Color B. Lay the legs out in an alternating color pattern. Tie them carefully to make a striped head. Then braid the legs by color, one leg in Color A, the next in Color B and so on.

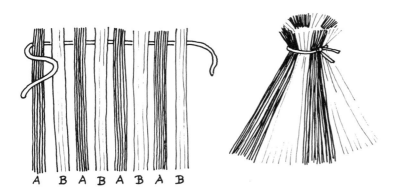

LARGE OCTOPUS: To make a large octopus you need two 4-ounce skeins of the kind of yarn sold 2 hanks to the skein. Cut each loop into 2 legs and put them together according to the regular octopus directions. This kind works very well in two colors.

One 4-oz. skein

•USE YOUR IMAGINATION . . .

Once you've learned the basic techniques you can begin to experiment with your own woolly animal ideas. Here are some sketches to help you get started.

III

HOOKED
AND RYA ANIMALS

This section is dedicated to people who can't resist big, furry animals. The Scottie is sturdy enough for a small child to ride, or you might want to tuck a tape recording of a ferocious barking into his tummy and use him as a guard dog. The llama is as tall as a three-year-old. The orangutan is here because I fell in love with one at the zoo about ten years ago; the anteater will satisfy whoever is looking for something unusual.

Hooking and Rya are combined in this book because both techniques create a "pile" effect, perfect for shaggy, cuddly animals. Many of the animals have easy-to-do crocheted or knitted features, but felt shapes can be substituted readily.

The techniques suggested to make the animals are latchet hooking and needle rya. Both are very simple to learn. Hooking allows you to use heavier yarn while rya makes it easier to blend yarn textures and colors. Because both are repetitive, they are easy to do without total concentration. The finished projects will last forever. If a hooking project is large enough, two people can work on it together, one working down from the top and the other working up from the bottom of the canvas.

Latchet Hooking

One of the nice things about latchet hooking is that you need just three things: yarn, a latchet hook and canvas. Only one kind of knot is used, whether you are hooking 1 or several strands of yarn at once.

Rya hooking is the same as regular hooking except that you normally work with longer strands of yarn, hooking 2 to 4 strands through the canvas mesh at once. Spaces of one or two rows can be left between the rows of rya to create a looser pile which lies down. If you do it every row, the yarn will stand straight up, just as with regular hooking. Regular hooking canvas is used.

You can follow the latchet hooking instructions for any of the rya hooking projects, but with all hooking, remember to pull the knots tight.

• MATERIALS

LATCHET HOOK: The two latchet hooks shown work in exactly the same way. There is a little latch below the hook which flips down to let you wind the yarn onto the hook easily and which flips up to hold (latch) the yarn in as you pull the yarn through the canvas. Shapes vary according to the manufacturer's design.

KNOT-HOOKING GUN: This is a hand-operated machine which works on the same principle as the latchet hook but much faster.

YARN: For projects which are not going to be walked on, (in other words, most of the animals) any type of yarn can be used effectively. If you want to work with a yarn which is lighter in weight than rug yarn, hook 2 to 4 strands at a time. Don't let the fact that pre-cut yarns are sold in 2¼" to 3½" lengths limit your ideas about how long the pieces should be. You can hook strands as long as you want. The only consideration is that the longer they are, the more time it takes to pull them through the canvas. The extra length can be a little awkward to work with. If you want to create a design with lots of long strands, you might prefer to use the needle rya technique. Remember, you can do needle rya right on the same canvas mesh along with hooking.

Keep each color and length of yarn in a separate plastic bag. It will save you a lot of time sorting.

Preparing yarn for hooking depends on how the yarn is packaged.

PRE-CUT PACKETS: Most pre-cut packets have approximately 320 to 360 strands, an average of 2½" in length. A pre-cut packet covers an area slightly larger than 4" x 8" on #3 or #3½ canvas. Rya yarn also comes in pre-cut packets, containing about 500 strands and averaging 3½" in length.

RUG YARN BY THE SKEIN: 1 ounce of uncut rug yarn will cover about the same area as 1 ounce of pre-cut rug yarn, but it does cost less than pre-cut packets. Rug yarn comes in wool and synthetic fibers. Wool is more expensive than synthetics but it looks best and wears best. A 70-yard skein of rug yarn will give enough 2½" lengths to cover an area 10" x 10".

LIGHTER WEIGHT YARNS BY THE SKEIN: Work with them the same as you would with the rug yarn but use more strands at a time. One reason you might want to use a lighter weight yarn would be if you couldn't get the color you wanted in a rug yarn.

TO MAKE YARN LENGTHS FROM LOOPED SKEINS: If the yarn comes in looped skeins, you are in luck. Cut the loops in half and then cut the halves into the lengths you want to use. Rya yarn comes in looped skeins. A rough guideline for measurement is that it takes one 100-gram looped skein per square foot using a 3-strand knot. One 25-gram skein gives about fifty-six 3-strand knots. In rya terminology, four 25-gram skeins together are called a hank.

TO MAKE YARN LENGTHS FROM CONES AND WOUND SKEINS: Find a strip or tube of wood, plastic or cardboard which is as big around as the length of yarn strand you want. Rulers and paper towel tubes

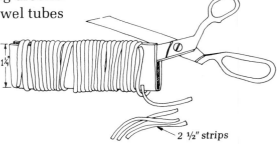

2 ½" strips

work very well. Wrap the yarn around the gauge from one end to the other and then cut the yarn once. You'll have a nice pile of strands the same length. Cones sold by the pound are usually a good buy. Remember that after the strand is hooked through the canvas, it will be half its original length.

WOOL CUTTER: This is an inexpensive machine that cuts yarn to desired lengths as you turn a handle. Check to see that it will make the lengths you want.

CANVAS: Plain rug canvas is sold by the yard and comes in several different widths, including 21″, 24″, 27″, 36″, 40″, 42″ and 48″. Mesh sizes vary from 3-squares-to-the-inch to 5-squares-to-the-inch. The smaller the squares, the lighter weight the yarn has to be to give a thick pile. For example, 3½-mesh-per-inch calls for 5- to 6-ply yarn and 4-mesh-per-inch is usually done in 3-ply rug yarn. ''Plain'' means there is no pre-painted design on the canvas.

NEEDLE: You'll need a good, heavy-duty carpet or yarn needle. Packets of needles are sold with straight and curved needles for repairing carpets, tents and upholstery. They are excellent for these projects. Or get a size #13 needle.

THREAD: Use a heavy-duty thread, such as buttonhole thread, for sewing animals together.

WHITE GLUE: A good, heavy-duty white glue like Elmer's or Sobo is needed for sealing all edges of the animal so they won't unravel when you sew them together.

STUFFING: Polyfill, cotton batting, rags.

• HOW TO USE A LATCHET HOOK

The hook can be held in the left hand or the right hand. You can work from left to right or right to left. Usually right-handed people prefer to work from left to right, holding the hook in the right hand. Left-handed people tend to work from right to left, holding the hook in the left hand. If you are working from the bottom of the design up, use Knot #1. If you are working from the top of the design down, use Knot #2. That way, all the knots will be facing in the same direction. It is best to work in rows but you can work on the canvas in different areas. When working with long strands, it's easier not to have to hook under a completed row. If you are following a curved line, work the knots along the pattern as if the curve were actually drawn like a series of steps.

KNOT #1: For working from the bottom of the design up.
    Fold yarn or yarns around hook.

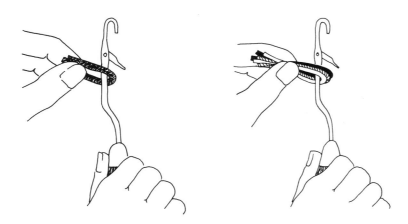

Push hook and latchet into one square and up through the square above. The latchet will open as it is pushed through. If it closes, open it with your forefinger.

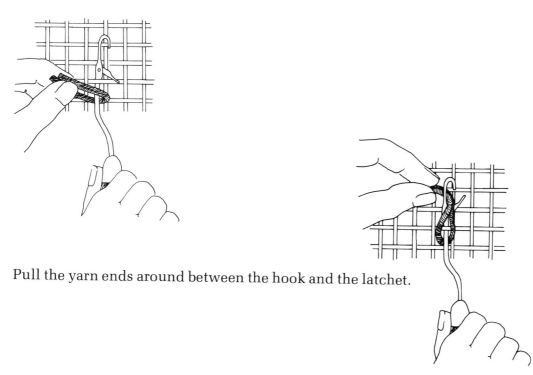

Pull the yarn ends around between the hook and the latchet.

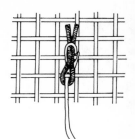

Pull the hook back out of the canvas. The yarn ends will automatically be pulled through the yarn loop and knotted.

Give the yarn ends a tug to tighten the knot. The knot loop will be toward you.

KNOT #2: For working from the top of the design down.

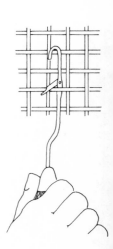

Push the hook into one square and up through the square above.

Fold the yarn in half and catch it with the hook.

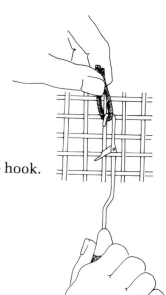

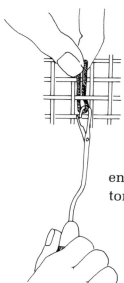

Holding the yarn ends, pull the hook back just far enough so that the yarn loop comes through the bottom square.

Without removing the hook from the loop, push the hook and latchet up and catch the yarn ends with the hook.

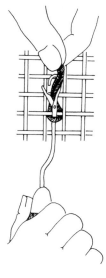

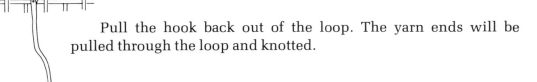

Pull the hook back out of the loop. The yarn ends will be pulled through the loop and knotted.

Give the yarn ends a tug to tighten the knot. The knot loop will be facing away from you.

Latchet hooking can be done by 2 people working together.

The girl above is making Knot #2.
This is what it looks like to her.

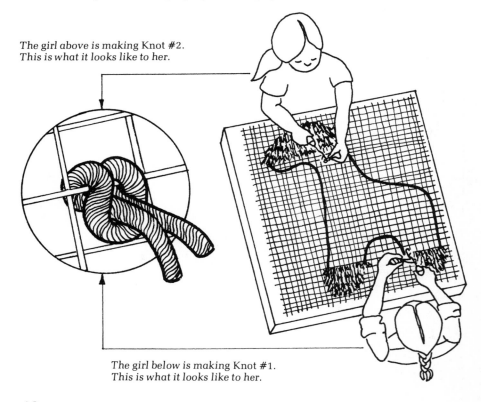

The girl below is making Knot #1.
This is what it looks like to her.

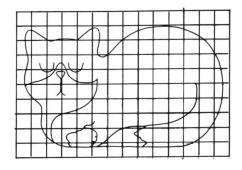

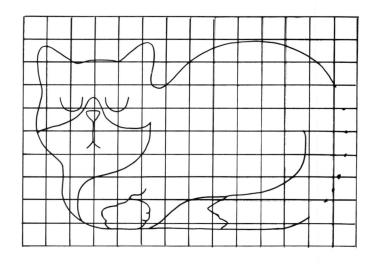

• OTHER TECHNIQUES

TRANSFERRING A PATTERN: Draw a grid of 1″ or 2″ squares on the mesh canvas using a waterproof marker. The size of the squares depends on the size of the pattern and the amount of detail. Copy the design from the pattern onto the grid by marking the points where the outline crosses the matching grid lines on the pattern. Then connect the points. (See illustration above.)

PREPARING THE CANVAS: Make a *very* heavy line with white glue all around the outline of each animal pattern piece. It is important that the glue line is solid. Otherwise the canvas will come apart when you cut the animal out and start to sew it together.

HOOKING THE ANIMAL: Follow the instructions on "How to Use a Latchet Hook" (p. 58). Make sure all your knots are facing in the right direction. Remember, you may have drawn the pattern pieces in different directions to fit them on the canvas. Mark each piece so that you know which is the top and bottom of the pattern. Don't forget to pull the knots tight!

SEWING HOOKED ANIMALS TOGETHER: Cut the hooked pattern pieces out, cutting just on the outside edge of the glue line. Then sew the animal together right-side out (unless otherwise specified) using a heavy needle, straight or curved, and buttonhole thread.

JOINING TWO PIECES OF CANVAS: If the piece of canvas isn't long enough for the pattern, you can join two pieces of canvas together. Overlap the mesh edges to be joined by about 2″. (See illustration.) Stitch both edges down with heavy thread. Make sure the mesh holes match over each other so you can hook through the two layers easily. The only thing to watch when you're adding on pieces of canvas is that you don't join them at a point in the pattern which has to bend. The joint will be too stiff.

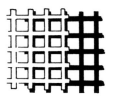

The Projects

• LADYBUG

The ladybug can be made any size, small for a pillow or large for a rug. The pillow is an ideal hooking project for a child to do, or for someone who wants to find out what hooking is like. Easy variations are the hedgehog, turtle and bear.

Pillow

MATERIALS
> 4 oz. red rug yarn, skein or pre-cut
> 3 oz. black rug yarn, skein or pre-cut
> Bits of white rug yarn or tripled white knitting worsted
> 15″ x 18″ rug canvas (#3, #3⅓, #3½, or #4)
> 15″ x 18″ black fabric for underbelly
> Waterproof marker
> White glue
> Stuffing—anything but foam bits

Transfer pattern to canvas. Run heavy glue line around outline. Hook design. Cut ladybug out, leaving a 1″ border. Hem down border to back. Cut out underbelly. Sew to edge of ladybug and stuff.

Rug

MATERIALS
> Rug canvas cut to size you want
> Enough yarn to cover canvas
> Rug tape or hem tape to go around edge of rug

Transfer pattern to canvas. Run heavy glue line around outline. Hook design. Trim the bare canvas at the glue line. Fold tape over the cut edge and sew it on. Then hem it to the underside of the rug.

64

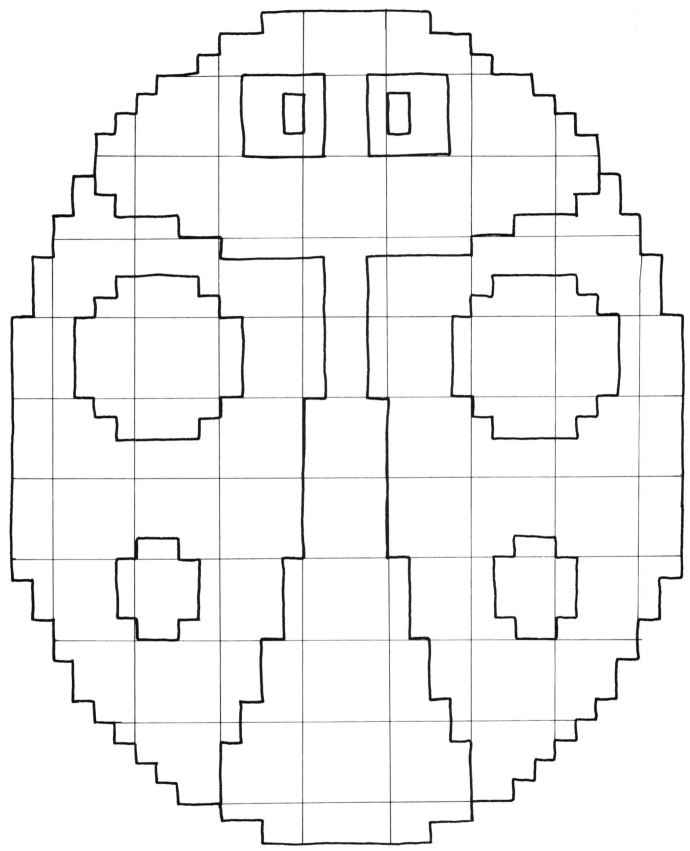

Scale: Each square represents 1″ square.

Variations

HEDGEHOG: Make same as ladybug, covering entire back area in mixed browns and beiges. Make strands on back twice as long as strands on head.

TURTLE AND BEAR: These two are suggestions to work out yourself.

• SCOTTIE

Here's a sturdy little life-sized fellow who's destined to be somebody's best friend. Make him in solid black, solid white, shades of gray and white, shades of beige and white or shades of blue-gray and gray. The Scottie made for this book is solid black, but you might want to combine colors. Check some pictures of Scottish terriers and similar dogs for color suggestions. This project can be completed with felt or crocheted ears, tongue and tail.

MATERIALS

  Latchet hook

  Rug yarn in colors of your choice—15 packets pre-cut rug yarn
  plus 16 oz. uncut rug yarn, or a total of 32 oz. uncut rug yarn

  #3⅓ mesh rug canvas, 27″ x 36″

  Cotton batting or rags for stuffing, 6 to 8 lbs.

  Buttons for eyes, if you want them (2 big white ones and 2
  smaller black ones for centers)

  Waterproof marker

  Felt pieces or other black fabric for soles of feet

  Heavy-duty curved needle

  White glue

  Plaid fabric if you want to make a tam and collar

  Red rug yarn (or other red yarn), bits for tongue and pompom
  on tam

  #K crochet hook (if you want to crochet the ears and tail)

Transfer the design to canvas using waterproof marker. Since
the lines are all straight, it is easy to draw the pattern onto canvas
with a ruler, counting squares and using the canvas threads as a
guide. There are two things which must be indicated on the
canvas: the length of the yarn strips in each area (short or long) and
the direction of the knots. Follow the key given with the chart . If
you are using Knot #1, draw arrows which will point toward you
while you are hooking. If you are using Knot #2, hooking should
be done with arrow pointing away from you.

Draw a *heavy* glue line *on* the outline of the pattern pieces. It
must be thick and solid! Otherwise the canvas mesh will fall apart
when you cut the pieces out.

Prepare the short and long lengths of yarn. Keep them in separate plastic bags. Use pre-cut packets for the short lengths or use a
ruler or other gauge which will give you 2½″ lengths. Use whatever
gauge will give you 5″ lengths for the long pieces. A paper towel
tube works well.

Hook the pattern.

Cut the pieces out, just outside the glue line. Run another glue
line around the cut edges for good measure.

Using a curved needle, sew the lower half of the body (legs,
sides and felt feet) together wrong side out. Turn right side out.
Stuff, then whipstitch top seams together.

Crochet a tail out of rug yarn or make a short, thick braid for
the tail. Make ears out of a double thickness of felt, or crochet ears
out of rug yarn (see below). If you want eyes, sew on buttons under
long eyebrows. Crochet a tongue or make one out of red felt and
sew it on.

See crochet directions, pp. 198–203

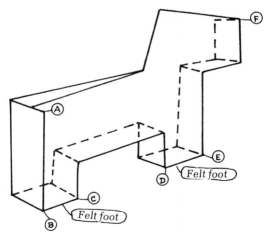

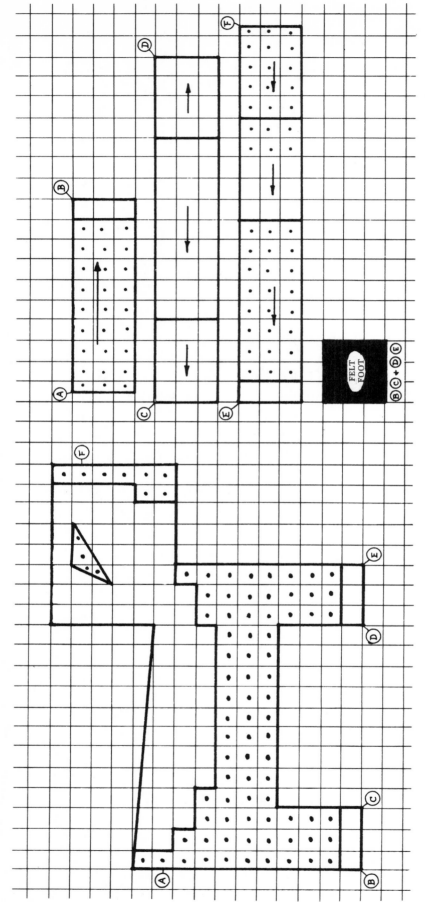

Make 2 of main body, one reversed.

Make 2 feet.

Each square = 1"

☐ = Square to be hooked in 2½" lengths of yarn.

• = Square to be hooked in 5" lengths of yarn.

↑ = Using Knot #1, hook with the arrow pointed toward you.

FELT FOOT

EARS

Make 2. Use black rug yarn and #K hook. Ch 10. Turn. Sc across (9 sc.) Ch 1. Turn.

Rows 2–3: Sc across. Ch 1. Turn.

Rows 4–6: Skip 1st sc. Sc across. Ch 1. Turn.

Rows 7–10: Skip 1st and last sc. End off and sew to head using curved needle and buttonhole thread.

TONGUE

Use red rug yarn or doubled knitting worsted and "K" hook. Ch 6. Turn. Sc across. Ch 1. Turn.

Rows 2–3: Skip 1st sc. Sc across. Ch 1. Turn. End off. Attach to head same as ears.

TAIL

Work in black rug yarn. Ch 12. Sl st tog. Sc around for 2 rnds. Dec 1 every other rnd for 7 rnds. Then dec 2 every rnd for 3 rnds. End off and attach same as ears.

TAM-O'-SHANTER PATTERN

Add a plaid tam to make your Scottie look really authentic. Cut a 12″ circle out of plaid fabric. Run a gathering stitch around the outside edge and draw it in to make it puff. Make a matching pompon and sew it to the center of the tam. Then sew the tam to the Scottie's head. If you want a removable tam, make a band to fit the gathered part.

COLLAR

Sew a matching plaid band around the Scottie's neck.

Needle Rya

Don't be put off by needle rya just because you've never seen it done before. Check the instructions. It's faster and easier than hooking and, because you are working on cloth rather than on canvas mesh, it is easier to sew the pieces of the animals together. Even though the Scottie, ladybug and bear are listed as hooking patterns, they work up just as well and faster in needle rya.

Hooking allows you to use heavier yarns; rya gives you an excellent opportunity to try something new with texture and color. Because you will be working with 2 or 3 strands of yarn at one time, you can mix colors. Try blending different colors and different textures. Thread the needle with both 2 strands of one color and 1 strand of another to create a tweedy, mottled or blended effect. Or thread the needle with three different colors. Or add a strand of a different texture yarn. You can create a blended or shaded effect by starting out by using 3 strands of one color. Then use 2 strands of the first color and 1 strand of another color too. Then use 1 strand of the first and 2 of the second. End with 3 of the second. Try mixing colors that are closely matched shades of the same color or try colors that are strong contrasts.

Needle rya done on burlap or other coarse material is very fast and simple. All you need to learn is a single stitch. And you end up with wonderfully soft, shaggy fur.

MATERIALS

YARN
Rya yarn is 2-ply, 100% wool and has a rope-like twist. You can use any yarns which allow you to thread 2 or 3 strands through the fabric backing without shredding the yarn or stretching the fabric out of shape. Some possibilities are:

fingering-weight yarn—great for extra-soft fur

70

baby yarn—also great for extra-soft fur

sport yarn—excellent for all-purpose use, plus good color selection

knitting worsted—good color selection; mix with lighter weight yarns

weaving yarn—retains the look of individual strands rather than blending together

thin rug yarn—also retains the look of individual strands rather than blending together, and is very strong; sold by the cone

string—mix with yarn or use alone for special effects

bulky, craft, quickpoint and rug yarn—use on very loose weave fabric, #5 double mesh canvas or rug canvas

How Much Yarn to Buy? Although it varies considerably, depending on how long you make the loops, how many strands you use, and how small or large you make your knots, 4 ounces or 100 grams of lightweight or rya yarn will cover approximately one square foot. Some books estimate that you can use up to 21 ounces or 600 grams to cover a square foot. I don't use that much, probably because I make relatively large knots and widely spaced rows which work perfectly well for the animals.

Fabric Backings: Choose from heavy burlap (14-ounce or heavier, though lighter will do; burlap comes in 54″, 58″ and 60″ widths); monk's cloth—expensive but beautiful to work with; hardanger cloth, or any similar fabric that is sturdy, slightly heavy, has a loose weave and doesn't come apart when a needle threaded with several strands of yarn is pulled through it.

Needles: Use a blunt tapestry, quickpoint or yarn needle with an eye large enough to thread with all the yarn you want to use. The average needle would be about #13; good needle sizes range from #10 to #16. A #10 has the largest eye. The new plastic needles work well with rya. If you work with a plastic needle, rya is a safe, easy project to do when you have small children climbing all over you and demanding constant or instant attention. Rya done with a plastic needle on #5 double mesh canvas is an excellent project for small children to do themselves.

• HOW TO DO THE RYA STITCH

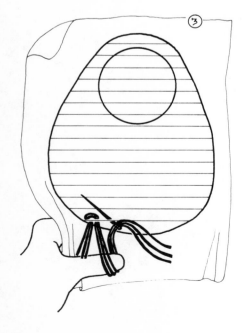

Pattern outlines

stitch guide lines

If your rya project is large, it may be easiest to work at a table.

Start in the lower left corner of each of your pattern pieces. (Remember, you may have drawn some of the pieces upside down to fit them on the fabric.) Work the stitches across and up, from left to right and row by row from bottom to top. You can work different sections that will be side by side as long as you don't have to sew one row of loops under another row. If you do, the loops will tend to get tangled. It is hard to do a row under another row, but not impossible.

1. Make a short stitch from right to left at the bottom left corner of your guide line. (If you are using burlap or monk's cloth, go under 2 or 3 threads.) Pull the yarn through, leaving a tail the length you want the loops to be.

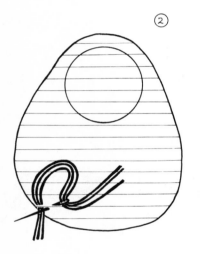

2. Then make another short stitch from right to left just to the right of the first stitch. (Your needle should come up through the right corner of the first stitch.) Pull the yarn through.

3. Make another short stitch to the right of the last one. As you pull the yarn through, catch the loop with your thumb and let your thumb determine the correct length of the loop. You can vary the length of the loops as you wish. If you want all the loops to be exactly the same size, work around a ruler, length of wood or dowel that gives you the size loops you want. Pass the yarn under and around the gauge between each knot.

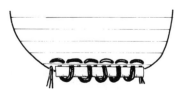

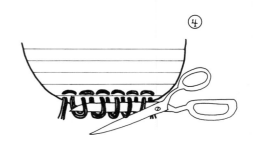

4. If you want a shag effect rather than loops, cut the rows after you have completed each row or every few rows. Irregular cutting creates a more shaggy effect.

Where rya rows change direction—for example, on the anteater's back—the yarn will hang down on either side. Where the rows meet, make sure the knots back up against each other, or run a loose back stitch the length of the row to make a neat folding point. Use the same yarn you used for the loops.

TURKEY TUFTING

When the rya stitch is done on #5 double mesh canvas, it is called Turkey Tufting. This works very well and it's easy to keep track of what you're doing. Leave every other row of the canvas empty unless you want the tufting to be extremely thick. Check the needlepoint section for instructions on how to do the Turkey Tufting stitch if you're not sure about how to do rya on mesh canvas.

Sometimes on mesh canvas the squares don't work out exactly right. You may come to a point where there isn't another hole for the knotting loop, either at the edge of the design or where there is a color change. If that happens, just pull the yarn through the back of the canvas and cut it off. Then it is anchored as well as if you had completed the stitch.

CONTROLLING PILE DENSITY: The more strands threaded on a needle at once, the denser the pile. You probably won't be able to use more than 3 strands with the types of fabric backing listed. I recommend that you work with a doubled thickness of yarn (2 strands folded in half), so you'll have 4 strands in each knot.

To make pile denser:
Use more strands of yarn.
Make smaller knots, more knots per inch.
Make rows closer together.
Use a soft yarn.
Brush the yarn.

How long should the loops be? They can be any consistent length, as short or as long as you like, but it is important to keep your rows close enough together so the fabric doesn't show between them. Remember, the rya will stick out when the animal is stuffed, so rows of loops must overlap. Needle rya is a good technique to use when you want extra-long loops.

There is a tendency to start out making the loops the same length as the instructions call for and then to make the loops smaller and smaller as you go along. The reason is simple. The shorter the loops, the farther the yarn will go before you have to thread the needle again. Everything goes faster and before you know it the project is finished. But then when the animal is stuffed, the yarn strands stick out instead of lying flat and the fabric is exposed. If that happens to you, just add rows of rya between the rows you have done already, or run a loose back stitch with several strands of yarn between rows. If you really have trouble keeping the loops long enough, cut a piece of cardboard about 12" long and as wide as you want the loops to be. Work the yarn around the cardboard row by row. This is a lot of unnecessary extra work; it is easier just to be careful to keep the loops uniformly long in the first place.

Line spacing for rya rows: Rya stitches can be done along straight or curved lines. Most of the stitching in these patterns follows straight lines. You can determine where the rows go by counting threads in the weave or by drawing stitch guide lines across pattern pieces.

When a project calls for rows to be spaced every ½", that doesn't mean you should skip the top line of the pattern just because it is only ¼" from the last row. Sometimes rows have to be closer to finish a pattern properly. Adjust the spacing whenever necessary.

It's impossible to give a rule about how to space lines to create specific effects. It depends on how long the loops are, what kind of yarn you are using and what size knots you are making. In general, if you make the rows ¼" apart you'll end up with a dense pile. If the rows are ½" apart the fur will be shaggier. If the rows are ¾" to 1" apart the fur will be very loose and may lie flat against the body. The farther apart the stitch lines are, the longer the loops must be to cover the fabric backing completely.

WORKING WITH A PATTERN

Any of the following methods will work.

METHOD 1: Draw a grid of 1" or 2" squares on the fabric. Copy the design from the pattern onto the grid by marking the points where the outline crosses the grid lines. Connect the points. (See illustrations on p. 63.)

METHOD 2: If you're nervous about drawing on the fabric directly, draw the design on tracing paper. Rub dressmaker's chalk over the lines on the back of the paper, or use dressmaker's carbon. Pin the drawing on top of the fabric and trace over the lines with a blunt pencil. Since the chalk lines will rub off, go over the lines in pencil or permanent marker. Carbon lines may not need to be traced over.

METHOD 3: Draw the pattern on tracing paper, then pin it to the fabric every inch or so and turn the fabric over, pattern-side-down. Draw a line connecting the pin points. Then, if you need a reverse of the pattern piece, pin the pattern to the back side of the fabric and do the same thing.

METHOD 4: Draw the pattern on tracing paper, then pin it over the fabric at the corners. Poke holes through the paper along the outline using a sharp marker or ballpoint pen, making a dotted outline of the pattern. Draw a line connecting the dots.

Notes: You can substitute newspaper or tissue paper for tracing paper.

Draw all pattern pieces on the fabric, allowing room for at least a 1″ border around each piece.

SEWING THE ANIMAL TOGETHER

Although I have sewn the animals together right side out, it is a problem because the thread gets tangled in the yarn. I recommend you sew as much of the animal as possible together inside out. Remember that rya makes the animal very bulky so you'll need a big hole for stuffing. Stuff the animal with whatever you have available and sew shut. If the sewn edges show, run a loose back stitch along the edge in the same yarn you used for the loops.

PATTERN SUGGESTIONS

Consider making a rya animal using the needlepoint mouse or owl pattern. Or try mixing angora wool in with other yarns on the cat pattern. The Scottie hooking pattern would work well in rya. Or do rya on any simple animal pattern.

The Projects

• HEDGEHOG

A cuddly, quick project. The pattern is drawn to be used on double mesh canvas. If you want to work it on burlap, round out the edges in the pattern. This is an easy project for children to do.

MATERIALS

4 oz. rug yarn in a dark color or mixed colors for body
2 oz. rug yarn in a light color for face
Bits of black, white and red yarn for eyes, nose and mouth. You can use rug yarn or use 2 strands knitting worsted, doubled.
#5 double mesh (Penelope) canvas, 12" x 30"
Rug needle
Stuffing (Polyfill best)
White glue

Transfer pattern to canvas. Drizzle a heavy, continuous line of white glue around pattern outline.

Work in single thickness rug yarn. Do needle rya stitches every other row, except do them every row for eyes, nose and mouth. Make body loops long (1¼" to 1½") and make face and feature loops short (¾"). Clip loops or leave them looped, whichever you like.

Cut out the pieces about 1" outside the outline. Sew together inside out, leaving bottom edge open. Turn right side out. Stuff and sew shut.

HEDGEHOG, BEAR AND PONY

Hedgehog: Make 2, one reversed.

Pony and Bear: Make 2 heads, one reversed.
Make 2 ears.

Scale: Each square = 1″

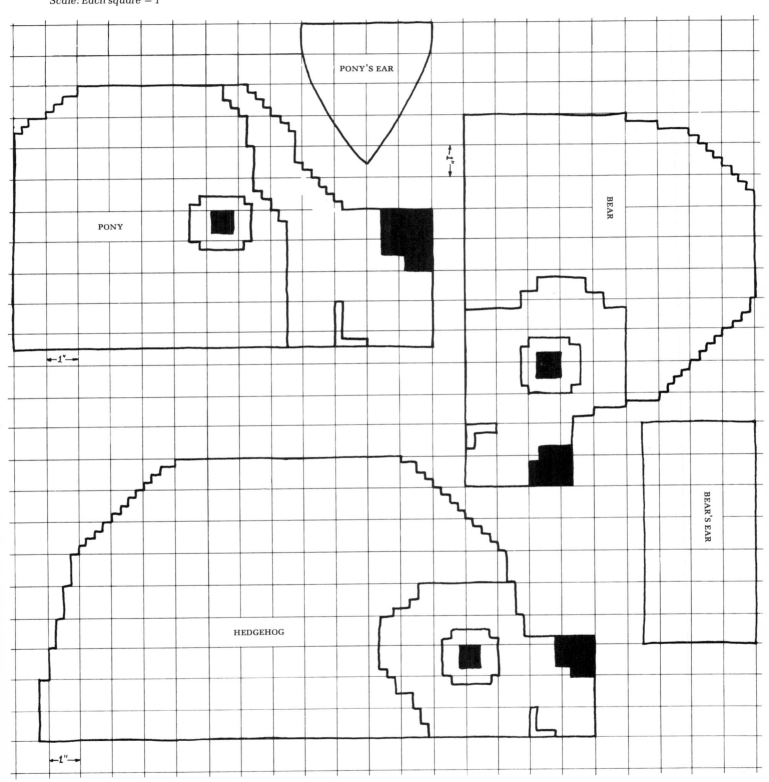

• BROOMSTICK BEAR (VARIATION ON HEDGEHOG)

For "bear-back" riding . . .

MATERIALS

    4 oz. rug yarn in dark color for back of head
    4 oz. rug yarn in light color for face and ears
    Bits of black, white and red yarn for eyes, nose and mouth. You can use rug yarn or 2 strands of knitting worsted, doubled.
    #5 double mesh (Penelope) canvas, 18″ x 36″ (or burlap)
    Rug needle
    Stuffing (Polyfill best)
    Furniture tacks (approx. 6)
    White glue
    Broomstick

Transfer pattern (see p. 63) to canvas or burlap. Drizzle a heavy white glue line around pattern outline if using mesh canvas.

Work in single thickness rug yarn. Do rya stitches every other row on canvas or every ½″ on burlap. Work every row for eyes, nose and mouth. Make loops about 1¼″ long. Clip loops or leave them looped.

Cut out the head pieces 1″ outside outline. Drizzle a heavy white glue line along bottom edge of both head pieces. Sew together inside out, leaving the entire top of the head open and a hole in the middle of the neck for the broomstick.

With face still inside out, stick broomstick through holes with head upside down (see illustration). Secure neck to broomstick 5″ from the top with tacks. Finish sewing neck shut if necessary.

Partially stuff an old sock. Stick the end of the broomstick in the sock and finish stuffing it. Tie the sock in place.

Turn the face right side out. Stuff and sew shut. Cut the ears out just outside glue line. Fold ear strips in half and sew sides shut. Sew ears to sides of head.

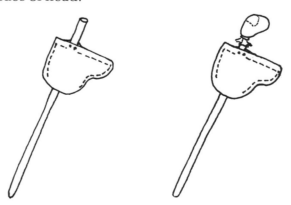

• BROOMSTICK PONY (VARIATION ON BROOMSTICK BEAR)

Although several adults have said this doesn't look like a pony, I took the pattern directly from a nine-year-old's sketch of her ideal dream pony.

MATERIALS

Use same supplies as for bear plus:

2 oz. rug yarn for mane, either in face color or a different color

Light color felt or other fabric to line ears

2 oz. contrasting rug yarn (for optional reins)

Follow same instructions as Bear, except for ears.

Cut ears out ½″ outside outline. Fold edges in and stitch felt pieces over them. Sew ears in place.

Make mane by doing several rows of rya stitching along the back of the head and up to the light blaze on the face. Make the loops 3″ or longer, depending on how you want the mane to look. Clip loops or leave them looped.

Reins are shown in the illustration.

One way to make reins is to crochet a circular chain in rug yarn to go around horse's nose. Slip stitch back along chain for strength. Then add a long chain (30″ or so) and join chain to opposite side of nose circle. Sl st back along chain for strength and end off.

• STAR-NOSED MOLE

I'd never seen a star-nosed mole before my cat brought one home. This little fellow has crocheted paws, nose and tail. You could design them out of felt very easily if you check the illustration. The original doesn't have eyes but you could attach little black shoe buttons just above his nose.

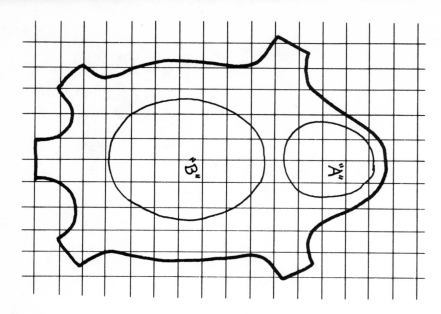

Each square = 1"
Make front and back for each animal.

MATERIALS

    2 oz. each sport yarn (or similar lightweight yarn) in light gray, light brown and beige
    2 oz. pink knitting worsted
    ½ yd. burlap, monk's cloth or other fabric for rya
    yarn needle
    #G crochet hook
    Stuffing (Polyfill best)

Transfer pattern to fabric. Mark horizontal lines every ½" from top to bottom on both pattern pieces. Add circle "B" from pattern for mole's belly to front pattern piece. (Do not use circle "A" for mole.) Do the rya stitch on the back side using gray and brown yarns mixed. Do rya stitch on front using mixed gray and brown around the outside, mixed light brown and beige inside that and finish the belly circle in beige. Make rya loops 1" to 1¼" long. Clip loops.

    Sew front and back together and stuff.

    Sew ends of legs, neck and tail shut.

    See crochet directions, pp. 198–203.

Paws: Make 4, using pink yarn and a #G hook. Ch 12. Sl st tog. Sc around.

    Rnds 2–4: Sc around, increasing 2 each rnd. (18 sc.)

    Rnds 5–6: Dec 2 each rnd.

    Rnd 7: Work even.

    Close the end of the paw in the following way: (Ch 4. Sl st back along ch to paw to make a claw. In next 2 sc sl st both sides paw tog) 5 times. End off. Stuff and sew to legs.

Nose: Using pink yarn, ch 2. Work 6 sc in 2nd ch from hook. Do not join. Mark beg of rows.

Rnd 2: 2 sc in each sc (12 sc).

Rnd 3: (Sc in 1st sc. 2 sc in next) around.

Rnd 4: Sc around, inc 4 evenly spaced. (22 sc).

Rnds 5–7: Work even.

Rnds 8–9: Inc 4 evenly spaced each rnd. (30 sc.)

Rnds 10–12: Work even. End off.

To add "star" to nose, go back to Rnd 4. Tie yarn on. (Sc, dc and tr in 1st sc. Tr, dc and sc in 2nd sc. Sl st in 3rd sc) around once and end off. Stuff and sew around "neck."

TAIL: Using pink, ch 12. Sl st tog. Sc around 6 rnds. Then dec 1 every other rnd until you run out of stitches or until you feel like the tail is long enough. End off. Stuff and attach.

Variations

Beaver and Duck-billed Platypus.

• BEAVER

A beginner's knowledge of crocheting is needed to make the beaver's head, paws and tail. If you really want to make a beaver but you don't want to crochet, study the illustration and the photograph and make the crocheted parts out of felt.

MATERIALS

2 oz. each sport yarn in rust, medium brown and dark brown
4 oz. dark brown knitting worsted
½ yd. burlap or other fabric for rya
Yarn needle
#G and #J crochet hooks
Stuffing (Polyfill best)
Bits of black and white yarn for eyes and teeth.

Transfer the pattern (same as mole, p. 79) to burlap. Add circles "A" and "B" to one side for face and belly. Mark horizontal lines every ½″ from top to bottom on both pattern pieces. Do rya stitch on back using dark and medium browns mixed. Do rya stitch on front using dark and medium browns around outside and blending medium brown and rust inside that. Finish with rust belly. (Do not stitch across face. Leave canvas blank.) Make rya loops 1″ to 1¼″ long.

Sew front and back together and stuff.

Sew ends of legs, neck and tail shut.

See crochet directions, pp. 198–203.

PAWS: Make 2, using dark brown knitting worsted and #G hook. Ch 12. Sl st tog. Sc around.

Rnds 2–4: Sc around, increasing 2 each rnd. (18 sc.)

Rnds 5–6: Dec 2 each rnd.

Rnd 7: Work even.

Close the end of paw in following way: (Ch 4. Sl st back along ch to paw to make a claw. In next 2 sc sl st both sides paw tog) 5 times to make fingers. End off. Stuff and sew to arms.

WEBBED FEET: Same as paws through Rnd 4.

Rnds 5–10: Sc around.

To close the end: (Sc and dc in 1st sc. dc and tr in 2nd sc. sc and sl st in 3rd sc) 3 times. End off. Stuff and sew to legs.

TAIL: Crochet with a doubled strand of knitting worsted and a #J crochet hook. Make 2. Ch 8. Dc in 2nd ch from hook and dc across. (7 dcs.) Ch 2. Turn.

Rnds 2–6: Dc across. Inc 1 dc each row in the middle. Ch 2. turn. (12 dcs.)

Rnds 7–11: Dec 1 dc each row. End off.

Slipstitch the two tail pieces together and sew to the back of the beaver. Do not stuff.

HEAD: Use knitting worsted and a #G hook. Ch 2. Work 6 scs in 2nd ch from hook. Do not join. Mark beg of rows.

Rnd 2: 2 scs in each sc. (12 scs.)

Rnd 3: (1 sc in next sc. 2 scs in next sc) around. (18 scs.)

Rnds 4–6: Sc around; inc 4 scs evenly spaced each rnd. (30 scs.)

Rnd 7: Sc around; inc 3 evenly spaced. (33 scs.)

Rnds 8–13: Sc around.

Rnd 14: (1 sc in next sc, dec 1) 11 times. (22 scs.)

Rnd 15: (1 sc in each of next 4 scs. dec 1) 7 times. (14 scs.) End off. Add eyes, nose, teeth and ears before you stuff the head and sew it to the beaver.

EYES: Make 2 in white using #G hook. Ch 2. Sc 4 times in 2nd ch from hook. Sl st to join into a ring. End off. Sew to head using a large French knot or satin stitch in black.

NOSE: Satin stitch a nose to the face in black .

TEETH: Make 2 in white knitting worsted with #G hook. Ch 4. Turn. Sc across. Ch 1. Turn. Sc across. End off and sew narrow end to head. Pointed corner should be down and toward the middle.

EARS: Make 2, using brown knitting worsted. Tie yarn to head where ear belongs. Sl st 4 scs in a row onto head. Ch 1. Turn. Sc across for 2 rows (3 scs). End off.

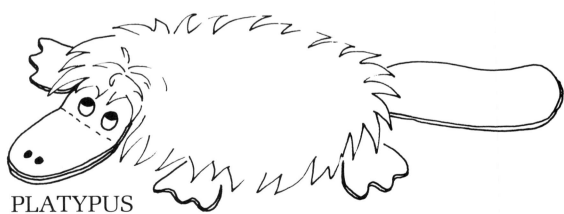

• DUCKBILL PLATYPUS

The duckbill platypus is included because someone looked at the star-nosed mole before he had his nose and said, "Are you making a duckbill platypus?" I checked the dictionary and came up with a wealth of information about the little Australian egg-laying aquatic mammal. "Platy" is Latin for flat and "pous" is Greek for foot. So here are the instructions on how to make a duckbill flat-foot with webbed feet and a beaver's tail.

MATERIALS
    2 oz. each sport yarn in light gray, light brown and beige
    4 oz. brown knitting worsted
    ½ yd. burlap, monk's cloth or other fabric for rya
    Yarn needle
    #G and #J crochet hooks
    Stuffing (Polyfill best)
    Bits of yarn and felt for eyes and nose

    Follow same rya instructions as for mole.

WEBBED FEET: Make 4, same as beaver webbed feet, in brown, using #G hook.

TAIL: Make same as beaver tail in doubled brown yarn, using #J hook.

FACE AND BILL: Make 2. Work in doubled brown yarn with #J hook. Make face same shape as Orangutan "Sole of foot" (p. 94). Stitch the 2 pieces together across the width, about ⅓ of the way down. Sew upper third around neck area. Leave lower ⅔ open for bill. Add eyes and nostrils of yarn and /or felt, as shown in illustration.

• LLAMA

The llama is a South American relative of the camel, who developed long hair instead of humps. It took a committee of four to put the original Lucy Llama together. Eleanor Hogg solved several problems by personally consulting a llama at the Toronto zoo. Did you know that llama tails look like over-sized rabbit tails? Mr. Hogg's efforts with coat hangers got Lucy to stand up. By stuffing her legs and body with rags for strength and by stuffing her neck and head with polyfill for lightness she became sturdy but not top-heavy.

    With all her problems solved Lucy is easy to reproduce. Her rya stitch fur goes quickly. Try to follow the instructions on how

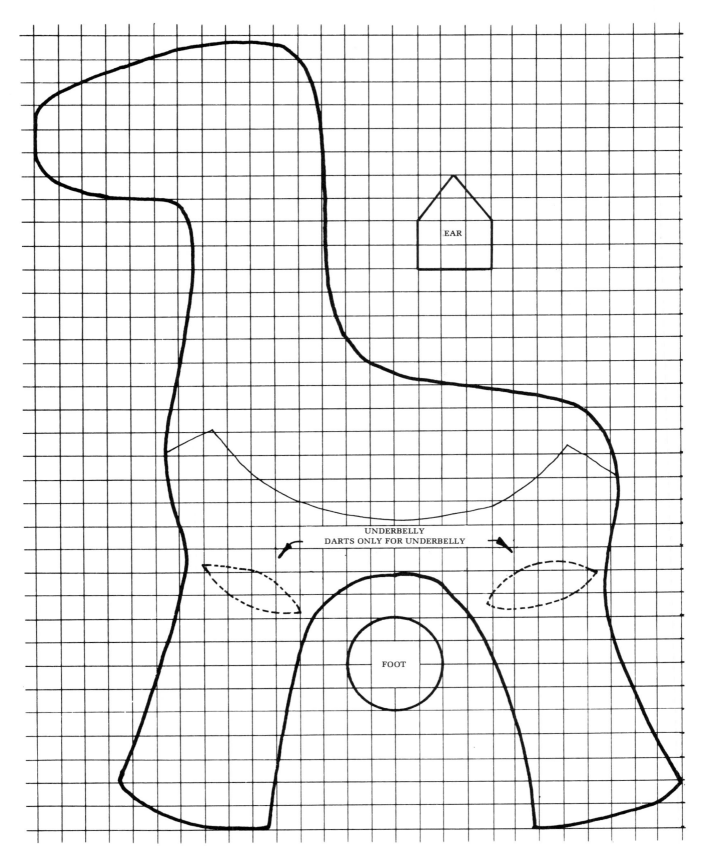

EAR

UNDERBELLY
DARTS ONLY FOR UNDERBELLY

FOOT

Body and Underbelly: Make 2 each, one reversed.

Scale: Each square represents 1″ square.

FOOT: *Make 4.*

EARS: *Make 2, felt or knitted.*

long to make the loops carefully for the most realistic results. Her ears can be made of felt or crocheted. The finished Lucy is as tall as a three-year-old and is a favorite with all ages.

Check knitting directions on pp. 164–170 if you are a beginner —the knitted ears are simple to make.

MATERIALS

Rya yarn, sport-weight yarn, weaving yarn or any combination of similar yarns (Phentex can be brushed to look like real llama fur):

8 oz. black

8 oz. brown (light and dark mix)

12 oz. white (white, off-white and cream or beige mix good, any combination)

1½ yds. burlap or monk's cloth

Yarn needle

Waterproof marker

Stuffing (rags and/or polyfill)—about 3 lbs. rags and 3 lbs. polyfill

Black felt for soles of feet

5 coat hangers

Wire cutters

2 long brown pipe cleaners (optional)

Felt bits or buttons for eyes

#5 knitting needles to make ears OR brown felt for ears

Transfer patterns to fabric. Make 2 each of the body and underbelly. Follow illustrations for horizontal stitch guide lines on body, for color chart and length of loops in different parts of body. Work stitches with 2 doubled strands of yarn.

When cutting out pattern pieces, either leave a 2″ seam allowance or run a glue line or machine-stitch line 1″ outside each pattern piece.

Sew body and underbelly together inside out, leaving upper part of back open. Turn right side out. Cut off hooks and bend coat hangers as shown in illustration. Partially stuff legs with rags and head with polyfill. Insert coat hangers and finish stuffing body and legs with rags and neck and head with polyfill.

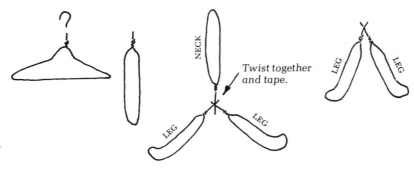

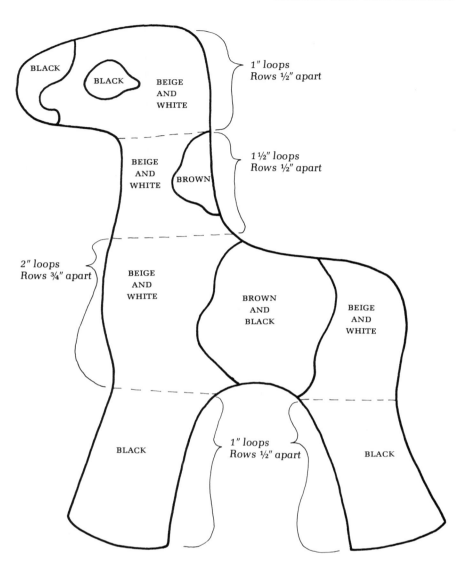

BLACK

BLACK

BEIGE
AND
WHITE

*1" loops
Rows ½" apart*

BEIGE
AND
WHITE

BROWN

*1½" loops
Rows ½" apart*

*2" loops
Rows ¾" apart*

BEIGE
AND
WHITE

BROWN
AND
BLACK

BEIGE
AND
WHITE

BLACK

*1" loops
Rows ½" apart*

BLACK

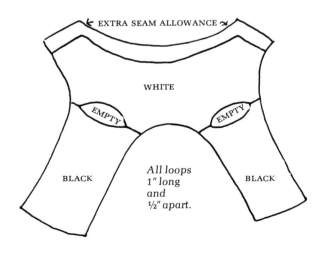

EXTRA SEAM ALLOWANCE

WHITE

EMPTY

EMPTY

BLACK

*All loops
1" long
and
½" apart.*

BLACK

87

KNIT EARS: Cast on 15 st. Knit 20 rows in stockinette stitch. Then knit 2 tog (decrease) at beg and end of every other row to 3 st. K last 3 tog and tie off. Sew ears on close together and so they stick up straight. Whipstitch the long brown pipe cleaners around the edges of the ears for extra stiffness (optional).

FELT EARS: Cut 4 out of brown felt and sew or glue them together in pairs. Sew ears on close together so they stick up straight.

TAIL: The llama's tail is like a rabbit's. Wind yarn (Phentex is especially good for this) around an 8"-wide piece of cardboard 50 to 100 times. Cut both edges. Tie tightly in middle and brush. Sew to back of llama.

Variations

ALPACA: An alpaca is just like a llama except it is all white. Make the loops in the body area extra long and fluffy.

GIRAFFE: Use the same pattern but add spots. If in doubt about placement, refer to a photograph of a giraffe. Make all the rows ½" apart and all the loops about 1" long. Add a mane all along the back of the neck. See other giraffe illustrations in Crewel section.

CAMEL: Use same pattern but add a hump. Check sketch of camel in Crochet section. Make all the rows ½" apart and all the loops about 1" long. Crochet ears like the ones in the sketch. Add a braided tail. Add long strands around hump and under neck, also seen in sketch.

• ANTEATER

Certain information is necessary to become a well-informed anteater owner. There are several varieties of anteaters. The pangolin is a scaly anteater from Asia and Africa who is able to roll into a ball when attacked. The aardvark is a large-eared, short-haired mammal from southern Africa. The echidna is a spiny Australian. The anteater shown here is the more popular *Myrmecophaga tridactyla* or giant anteater, sometimes referred to as the "ant bear." He is a tropical American mammal.

As a practical addition to any home, an ant trap would undoubtedly prove more valuable than this long-haired, scruffy fellow. But he is very loveable.

A little sewing and the rya stitch are all he needs. His face can be crocheted or made of fabric. If you want him to be straight-legged rather than floppy, check the llama instructions on how to add coat hangers to stiffen his legs. He's a lot of animal for the effort.

MATERIALS
   Rya yarn, sport-weight yarn, weaving yarn or any combination of similar yarns:
      4 oz. navy blue
      6 oz. blue-gray
      2 oz. gray (light)
      2 oz. white (or off-white)
   1 yd. burlap or monk's cloth
   Yarn needle
   Waterproof marker
   Stuffing
   Black or blue felt for feet
   Face—3 oz. blue-gray yarn and #G hook or ½ yd. blue-gray wool (use for feet, too)

Transfer pattern to fabric. Draw horizontal stitch guide lines on body every ½" for 4 rows in each direction coming out from the center fold. Then make rows every ¾" until you reach the legs. Make lines on legs and on underbelly every ½". Remember to change the stitch direction at center back so that the fur hangs down on either side of animal.

Work stitches with 2 doubled strands of yarn following the color chart. Loops should be 1½" long.

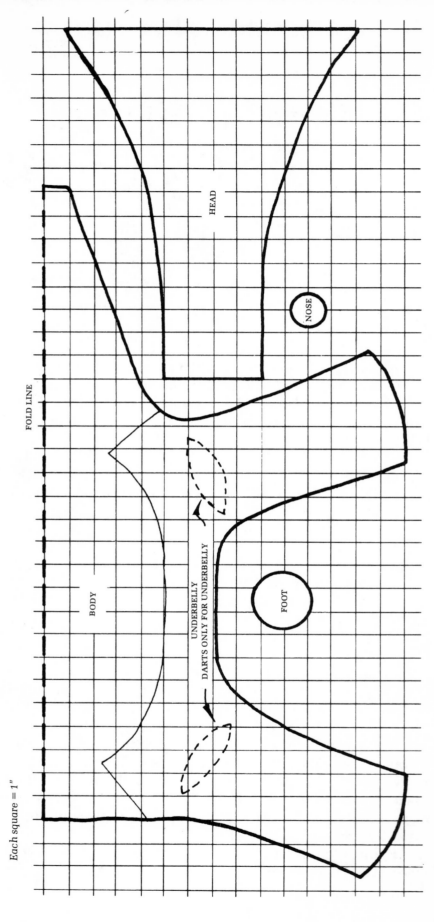

UNDERBELLY: *Make 2*   FOOT: *Make 4*

Each square = 1"

FOLD LINE

HEAD

NOSE

BODY

FOOT

UNDERBELLY
DARTS ONLY FOR UNDERBELLY

90

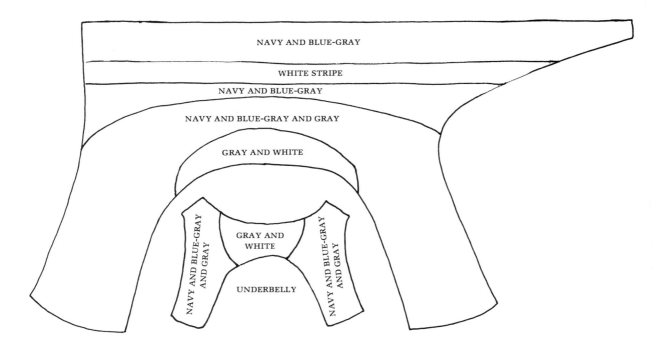

When cutting out the pattern pieces, either leave a 2″ seam allowance or run a glue line or machine-stitch line 1″ outside each pattern piece.

Sew body and underbelly together inside out, leaving entire front edge open. Turn right side out. Sew on feet. Stuff and sew up front to head opening.

Make the head. If you use fabric, cut out 1 head and 1 nose piece. Fold head in half lengthwise. Sew long seam and add nose. Stuff and sew to front of body as shown in illustration on p. 89. Add ears and eyes made out of fabric, felt or yarn.

If you crochet the head, single or double crochet the shape shown in the pattern. Crochet 2 strands together for strength, using any combination of leftover navy blue, blue-gray and gray yarns, to the shape shown in the pattern.

Note: See "How to Design Your Own Crochet Pattern" in Crochet section.

CROCHET EARS: Use doubled yarn in same color as head. Ch 3. Sl st tog. 7 tr in circle. Turn. Ch 2. (Dc in next 2 tr. 2 dc in next tr) repeating to end. End off and sew to head.

CROCHET EYES: Work in double thickness navy. Ch 3. Sl st tog. Make 7 sc in circle. End off. Sew to head using white yarn around edges to make a solid white outline.

Stuff and sew head to front of body same as for fabric head, above.

• ORANGUTAN

He's my special favorite, all arms and legs and love. His name comes from the Malaysian words *orang* (man) and *utan* (forest) and he's a native of Borneo and Sumatra.

Some crocheting is required to make his features unless you want to design features out of felt. Even though the shapes you have to crochet are somewhat unorthodox, you'll find they're easy to make if you follow the diagrams.

MATERIALS

Rya yarn, sport-weight yarn, weaving yarn or any combination of similar yarns:

   6 oz. orange
   4 oz. gold
   4 oz. rust
   2 oz. yellow

4 oz. beige or cream yarn, rug weight, for face, hands, feet, ears
#K crochet hook
Yarn needle
Waterproof marker
Stuffing (approx 2 lbs polyfill works well)
1 yd. burlap or monk's cloth (piece 30″ x 36″)

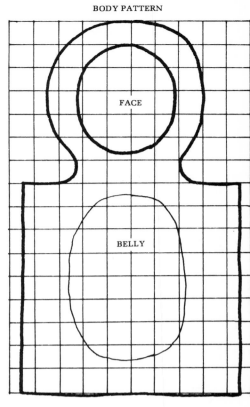

BODY PATTERN

FACE

BELLY

Make 2 body pieces. The back is just like the front but without face and belly.

Scale: Each square represents 1″ square.

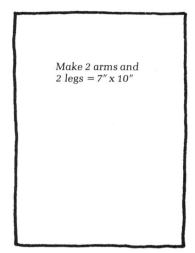

Make 2 arms and 2 legs = 7″ x 10″

Transfer pattern to fabric. You might want to run a glue line or machine stitch about ½″ outside each pattern piece to prevent possible fraying.

Draw in stitch guidelines. Mark concentric circles in the area around the face, leaving the face blank. Draw horizontal lines ½″ apart on rest of body and back. Draw lines ½″ apart across the 7″ width on the arms and legs.

Work stitches with doubled strands of yarn. Mix orange, gold and rust for body, arms and legs. Blend yellow and gold around edge of belly and do belly in yellow (or yellow and gold, if you prefer).

Sew the body pieces together right side out using yarn or heavy thread. Stitch arms and legs in as you go. Stuff body loosely. Wait to stuff arms and legs until hands and feet are made.

Use rug yarn and "K" hook.

FACE: Ch 4. Sl st tog. 2 sc in each ch around.

Rnds 2–3: (2 sc in 1st sc. 1 sc in next sc) around.

Rnd 4: Inc 4 evenly spaced.

Rnd 5: Sc around. Mark half-way point.

Rnd 6: Continue to sc. Dec 2 on 1st half. Sc other half.

Rnd 7: Inc 1 every other sc 1st half. Sc other half.

Rnd 8: Inc 1 every other sc 1st half. Sl st last sc in 1st half. Turn back and sc around same half.

Rnd 9: Turn and sc around same half.

Rnd 10: Sc around entire head. End off.

EARS: Make 2. Ch 5. Sc to end of ch. 4 sc in last ch. Sc back around other side of ch. 3 sc in each of 2 sc at end. Sc around other side. 3 sc in each of 2 sc at end. Sc around other side. Sl st at end and end off.

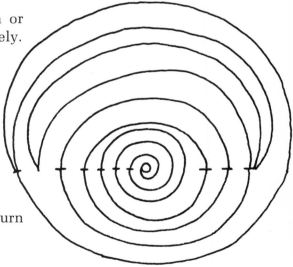

FACE

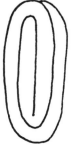

EAR

93

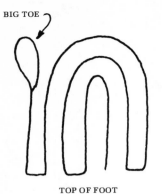

BIG TOE

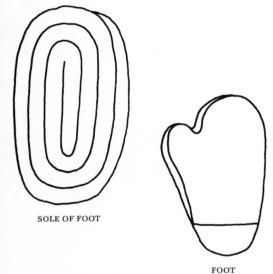

TOP OF FOOT

SOLE OF FOOT

HAND

FOOT

TOP OF FOOT: Ch 7. Sc in 2nd ch from hook. Sc to end. Ch 2. Turn. Sc to end. Sc 3 in last sc. Work around end. Sc 3 in 1st sc and sc down the other side. Ch 2. Turn. Sc around. Sc 2 in 6th, 7th, 8th and 9th sc and then sc to end. Ch 2. Turn. Sc in 1st 6 sc. Big toe starts here. Ch 3. Turn. Sc back and sl st into 6th sc. End off.

SOLE OF FOOT: Make 2. Ch 7. Sc to end. 3 sc in end ch. Sc down other side. 3 sc in end sc and in 1st sc on other side. Sc to end. 2 sc in 5th, 6th, 7th and 8th sc. Sc to end. 2 sc in 5th, 6th, 7th and 8th sc. Sc to end. Sl st next sc and end off.

TO PUT FOOT TOGETHER: Sl st sole to top, slip stitching around the big toe as you go around. Remember to make a left foot and a right foot.

HAND: Ch 11. Sl st tog. Sc around for 5 rows.
  Row 6: Dec 2.
  Row 7: Dec 2.
  Row 8: Sl st across top.
  Tie yarn on where the thumb would join the hand. Sc 7 in a ring to make the base of the thumb. Sc around 3 times, dec 1 each row. End off.

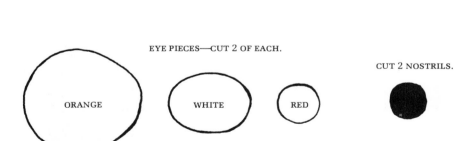

EYE PIECES—CUT 2 OF EACH.

CUT 2 NOSTRILS.

ORANGE

WHITE

RED

These sketches are full-size.

FINISHING: Stuff arms and legs softly. Stuff and sew on hands and feet. Sew face to space on head, stuffing it to hold shape. Sew ears to sides of head. Make features for orangutan using yarn and felt scraps (see illustration) or buttons.

94

Variations

Change the ears and faces and add tail to make different animals.

RABBIT: Make 2 ears following the rya beaver tail pattern. Add a large pompom tail.

DOG: Wide, floppy rya ears and a rya tail would turn the orangutan into a dog. You could also work even for several rows as you crochet the nose part of the face to make a longer dog's nose. You might want to leave thumbs and big toes off the hands and feet.

CAT: Crochet pointed ears and make a long tail, either crocheted or rya. You could also crochet little claws around the hands and feet, leaving off the thumbs and big toes. Use chain stitch for the claws, then slip stitch back along chain for strength.

• LION

The rya stitch and a little crewel will quickly complete our lion. Try making him the same size or bigger than the original needlepoint cat pattern. If you decide to make him bigger, remember to buy more yarn and a bigger piece of fabric and burlap. The face can be worked in crewel directly on the burlap using the yarns listed below.

MATERIALS

    2 ozs. each sport-weight yarn in pale gold, pale orange and bright orange
    1 oz. beige or white for the paws (or do them in one of the above colors)
    2 pieces of burlap, each 17″ x 13″
    1 piece of colorful fabric to match the yarn 17″ x 7″ (for bottom of cat)
    Yarn needle
    Stuffing

Transfer the pattern to burlap. Mark horizontal lines every ½″ from top to bottom on both pattern pieces except on the head area. Leave the part that will be the face blank and draw three circles

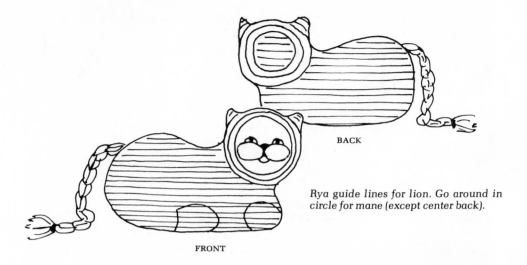

BACK

Rya guide lines for lion. Go around in circle for mane (except center back).

FRONT

around it. For the back of the head, draw concentric circles or draw two circles around the outside of the head with horizontal lines across the middle area. Do the rya stitch on the body in pale gold and pale orange mixed. Make the loops ¾" to 1" long. Make the loops for the paws the same, using beige or white yarn.

The circles around the face and back of head are for the mane. Work the circles around the face and the entire back of the head in bright orange or a mixture of both oranges. Make the loops 1½" to 2" long.

Work the face in crewel.

Cut the bottom piece out of fabric. Sew the lion together and stuff him.

Braid a tail out of a mixture of the yarns.

Variations

You could make an Angora cat from the same pattern by using angora or mohair-like yarn alone or mixed with baby or fingering yarn.

I • WOOLLY ANIMALS (top right, clockwise): Mini-Monster Friend, page 37; Loopy Lamb, page 48; Squeezable Squirrel, page 43; Mini-Cat (orange and yellow), page 52; St. Bernard Pup (brown and white), page 46; Octopus, page 49; Pompom Poodle Pup (yellow and white), page 41; Grouchy Lion, page 44; Panda Bear, page 40; Cuddly Caterpillar and Friend, page 38.

II • KNITTED ANIMALS (top left, clockwise): Multicolored Elephant (purple), page 174; One-color Elephant (green), page 174; Elephant Finger Puppet (pink and blue), page 180; Black-and-White Skunk, page 186; Octopus Finger Puppet, page 181; Two-color Porcupine, page 186; "Any-Animal" Cat Puppet, page 178; "Any-Animal" Dog Puppet, page 179. *See VII for more knitted animals.*

III • NEEDLEPOINT ANIMALS (top left, clockwise): Mouse, page 149; Cat, page 144; Owl, page 153; Elephant, page 156; Snail, page 142.

IV • CREWEL-EMBROIDERED ANIMALS (top, clockwise): Bird, page 114; Cat, page 122; Giraffe, page 116; Unicorn, page 118; Fish, page 112; Hippo, page 119.

V • CROCHETED ANIMALS (top, clockwise): Broomstick Dragon, page 217; Camel, page 220; Quick Kiwi, page 206; Walrus, page 215; Mr. Big-Mouth, see "Any-Animal" Puppet size, page 205; Turtle with Removable Shell, page 211. *See VIII for more crocheted animals.*

VI • HOOKED AND RYA ANIMALS (top center, clockwise): Broomstick Pony, page 79; Orangutan, page 92; Llama, page 84; Anteater, page 88; Ladybug, page 64; Beaver, page 81; Scottie, page 66.

VII • KNITTED ANIMALS (top left, clockwise): Owl, page 175; Rabbit, page 187; Dragon, page 192; Zebra, page 184; Pony (purple), page 183; Donkey, page 182; Mother Kangaroo and Baby, page 189. *See II for more knitted animals.*

VIII • CROCHETED ANIMALS (bottom left, clockwise): Turtle with Removable Shell (underview), page 211; Dragonflies and Butterflies, page 208; Pink Piggy Bag, page 210; Red, Brown and Blue Bookworms, page 207. *See V for more crocheted animals.*

IV

CREWEL-
EMBROIDERED
ANIMALS

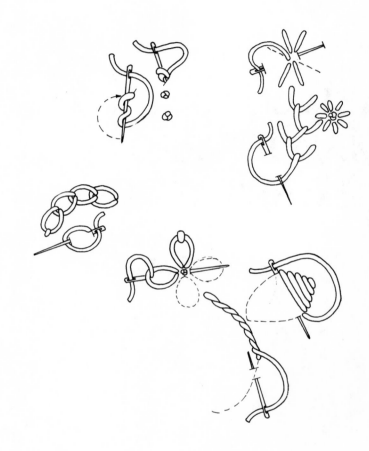

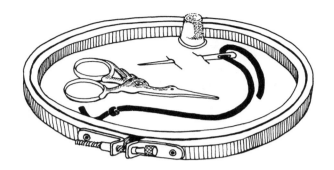

"Crewel" comes from a Middle English word, crule, which means a lightly twisted wool. It was a popular early American craft and its simplicity makes it very appealing today.

The Crewel section is devoted to the idea of the sampler. A sampler is a decorative piece of needlework made up of samples of a variety of stitches. It is a way to learn new stitches and to work on design variations of your own.

Patterns are given but think of them only as suggestions. Any fabric animal pattern can be decorated with crewel stitches. Remember that once the animal has a face, the amount of stitchery from then on is entirely up to you.

Patterns from the Needlepoint and the Hooking/Rya sections can be adapted to crewel easily.

General Directions

• CREWEL STITCHES

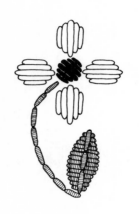

Crewel is marvelously quick and simple. There are hundreds of possible stitch variations to borrow from embroidery. But all you need to know is how to make a straight stitch and a loop. Everything else is a variation.

The flower illustration shows how the straight stitch can be used to create lines and fill in areas of color. With the straight stitch, you can create all kinds of wonderful, colorful pictures.

The loop offers more possibilities. The ends of the loop can come out of the same hole, or come out of holes right next to each other, or come out of holes that are far apart.

The loops can be left sticking out to create a fuzzy, raised effect.

Or the loop can be tacked down at one point, at two points, or at three or more points (called a crown stitch).

The tack stitches can be short or long, straight or looped or any combination.

The loops can be far apart or close together.

The combinations are endless.

100

Another way to create design variations is by threading or lacing stitches with the same color or different color yarns. It is a good way to use heavier yarns since the yarn is laced through the stitches and not through the material. The wonderful thing about threaded stitches is that they cover an area quickly and look so nice.

Note: You may know these stitches by different names.

Straight Stitch: The flower is made of straight stitches coming out from a French Knot (illustration p. 108) in the center.

Spider Stitch: A variation of a threaded flower.
Spider Web Stitch: A variation of a threaded flower.

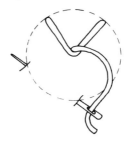

Fern Stitch: Another way to work straight stitches into a design.

Running Stitch: A line of evenly spaced straight stitches.

Double Running Stitch: A second line of running stitches is worked back between the original line of running stitches.

Darning Stitch: A line of running stitches done close together.

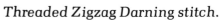

Threaded Zigzag Darning stitch.

101

Whipped Running Stitch.

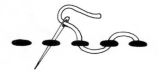

Laced Running Stitch.

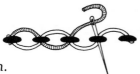

Double Threaded Running Stitch.

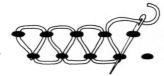

Threaded Checkerboard Running Stitch.

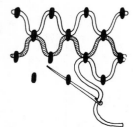

Wave Stitch.

Back Stitch: An excellent outline stitch.

Running Back Stitch.

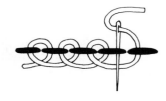

Pekinese Stitch.

Threaded Back Stitch.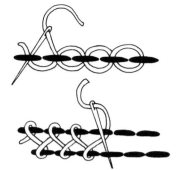

Interlaced Back Stitch.

Split Stitch: A back stitch with the needle passing back through the fabric and also through the yarn, splitting the yarn.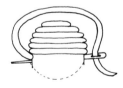

Stem Stitch: An overlapping back stitch.

Couching Stitch: Another way to make a line. Lay a piece of yarn on the fabric and stitch it down at regular intervals using a straight stitch, a cross stitch or any other stitch which might work. It's a good way to use a piece of yarn that is too heavy or too fragile to pull through the fabric.

Thorn Stitch: Couching done with a cross stitch.

Satin Stitch: Back stitches done right next to each other to fill in an area. The stitches can be worked horizontally, vertically or diagonally across the design. If you're having trouble making a neat edge, go over the outline first in a split stitch and then work the satin stitch over the split stitch.

Surface Satin Stitch: Like the satin stitch but it uses less yarn—and may not cover as well. Tiny stitches are made along the outline between satin stitches.

Fishbone Stitch #1: Another filling stitch.

Basket Filling Stitch.

Seed Stitch: Another way to fill in an area. Small single, double or triple stitches are scattered around. Spacing and size are up to you.

Long and Short Stitch: Another filler stitch in the satin stitch style. Alternate long and short stitches along the first row. Then fill in with long stitches until the last row where long and short stitches alternate again to create an even edge. A nice stitch to use if you want to blend colors. For example, work the first row in a dark color and then change to lighter and lighter shades as you work toward the last row.

Cretan Stitch: A filler stitch which works well as a border and also to fill in shapes like leaves.

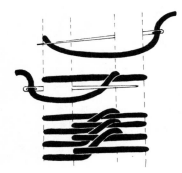

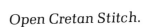

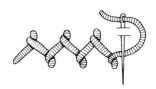

Open Cretan Stitch.

Cross Stitch: Two equal-length stitches crossing diagonally from opposite corners of a square.

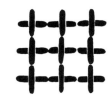

Upright Cross Stitch.

Trellis Couching: Long, crossed threads tacked down with cross stitches at intersections. Good variation for filling an area.

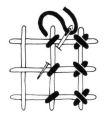

Cross Stitch Flower/Star.

Herringbone Stitch: Can be varied in spacing and color.

Threaded Herringbone.

LOOPED STITCHES
First read about loop variations in the introduction to crewel.
    Single Feather Stitch: An open loop.

Feather Stitch: Just like the blanket stitch (see illustrations p. 106) only with slanted stitches.

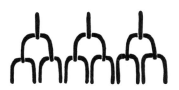

105

Scroll Stitch: Like the feather stitch but the yarn passes under the needle twice instead of once.

Cable Chain Stitch: One step beyond the scroll stitch. The yarn is wrapped around the needle and then under the needle.

Slanting Feather Stitch.

Fly Stitch/Threaded Straight Stitch.

Fishbone Stitch #2: Variation of fly stitch.

Blanket Stitch and variations.

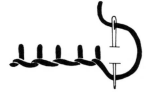

Double Blanket Stitch.

Buttonhole Stitch: Blanket stitch with stitches close together.

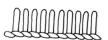

Chain Stitch.

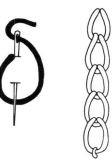

Checkered Chain Stitch: Thread the needle with two colors of yarn.

Open Chain Stitch.

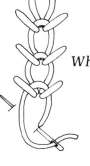

Wheatear Stitch.

Lazy Daisy Stitch: A circle of chain stitches.

Reverse Daisy Stitch.

Chained Feather Stitch.

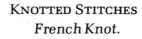

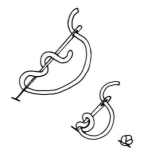

KNOTTED STITCHES
French Knot.

Bullion Knot: A long French knot.

Bullion Flower.

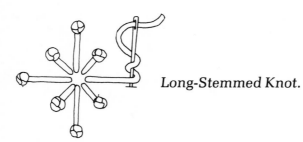

Long-Stemmed Knot.

YARNS FOR CREWEL
(General chart to give you ideas)

FINE	MEDIUM	HEAVY
(For light cotton and similar fabric)	(For fabric like linen and wool)	(For fabric like burlap, or attach to lighter fabric using couching stitches)
Embroidery floss	Crewel yarn	3- or 4-ply knitting worsted
Pearl cotton	Persian wool	Quickpoint yarn
Silk buttonhole thread	Tapestry yarn	Rug yarn
	Baby-weight yarn	Raffia
	Darning wool	Twine
	Metalic yarns	Jute
	Crochet cotton	Weaving wools
	String	

FOUR TRANSFER METHODS

Even if you want to do free crewel, following no definite pattern, there is an advantage to adding guide lines. They keep a straight line straight and a circle round. Four alternatives:

(1) The best way to transfer patterns is to draw the design on tracing paper first. Then use dressmaker's carbon to transfer the design to the fabric. Put carbon face down on fabric and pin the design on top of the carbon. Trace the lines with a blunt pencil. Handle carbon carefully so it doesn't smudge. Dressmaker's carbon comes in light and dark for different color fabrics. Don't use regular carbon paper!

(2) Draw the design freehand onto the fabric using a soft lead pencil, tailor's chalk or a chalk pencil. Watch that your lines don't come too close to the edges which will be seamed.

(3) For small patterns and thin fabrics this may work. Pin the fabric over the pattern. Hold them up together against a window and trace the design through.

(4) Another way to transfer pattern pieces to fabric is with a pink transfer pencil. To use the pencil, draw directly over the lines on the back of the tracing. With a medium-hot iron, iron the pattern, pink side down, onto the fabric. (especially helpful on dark fabrics)

• MATERIALS

NEEDLES

Embroidery needles: Long eye, sharp point. For delicate fabrics and cotton embroidery floss or separate strands of wool.

Tapestry needles: #16, #17 and #18—blunt-pointed for heavy, loose-weave fabrics and for threading yarn through stitches. Large eye.

Chenille needle: Like tapestry needle. Long eye.

Crewel needle: Sizes #1 to #12 (higher number for finer work). Size 3 or 4 is average. Long eye. Sharp point.

Yarn needle: For heavy, loose-weave fabric like burlap. Large eye. Blunt point. Size #18 is average. Size #13 is for very heavy yarns, like rug yarns.

Rug needle: For heavy, loose-weave fabric and very heavy yarns. Large eye. Blunt point.

Selecting a needle

The eye of the needle must be large enough for the yarn you want to use. The point should be sharp for tight-weave fabrics and blunt for loose-weave fabrics. A blunt-pointed needle is also good for threading and lacing stitches since it won't catch in the stitches that are being laced. If it's hard to pull the yarn through the fabric, causing the yarn to fray, switch to a bigger needle. It will make a larger hole in the fabric so the yarn can be pulled through easily. If the yarn is still too heavy and you really want to use it, try attaching it to the fabric with couching stitches.

Threading the needle

Most of the time, you can just stick the yarn straight through the eye. But there is a recommended technique which can be a lifesaver. Fold yarn around the needle and pull to make a crease. Carefully remove the creased fold from the needle and slip the fold through the needle eye or slide the needle over the fold.

Rusty needles

If the needle gets rusty, rub it lightly with fine sand paper or with a fine emery board, or push it in and out of the emery "strawberry" attached to most "tomato" pin cushions.

Fabric

If you can get a threaded needle through the fabric, you can use it for embroidery. Use a good quality fabric which will not be easily distorted by the crewel stitches and which will wear well. Linen, burlap, heavy cotton, wool or fabric blends are all good. A fabric with texture resembling linen or burlap provides a good background for the crewel yarns. Think about using colored fabrics and fabrics with patterns on them (stripes, polka-dots, checks) as a guide for your designs.

Embroidery hoop

See illustration p. 99. Two wood or metal hoops, round or oval, in many sizes. One hoop fits inside the other. The outside hoop usually has a screw so you can adjust it.

Although an embroidery hoop isn't essential, it is a big help. It holds the fabric taut and keeps the stitches neat and even. Without it you may pull the stitches too tight and the work will pucker.

If you don't have a hoop and can't wait to get started, spray the back of the fabric with spray starch and iron it to give it more stiffness.

SCISSORS

You'll need large scissors for cutting fabric and small, pointed scissors for cutting stitches in case of a mistake or change of mind.

PRESSING

To make the finished project look nice, the pieces should be pressed before the animal is sewn together.

Put crewel face down on a folded towel. Press lightly, using a damp cloth or you can spray starch for extra stiffness. Then press dry. Turn the work right side up and press the parts where there are no crewel stitches.

You can spray the animal with Scotchgard stain repeller to keep it clean.

• MAKING A CREWEL ANIMAL

Enlarge patterns to whatever size you wish on tracing paper. Draw a ½″ seam allowance all around the pattern pieces (except for the hippo, which has a ⅜″ seam allowance already included in the pattern). Pin the tracing paper pattern to the fabric and transfer the pattern in the method of your choice.

Do all the crewel work. Press the fabric.

Then cut the pieces out along the seam allowance lines. Sew pieces together inside out as indicated in the pattern. Leave an opening at the rear or bottom of the animal. Clip curved seams.

Turn the animal right side out. A big crochet hook or the eraser end of a pencil is good for poking legs out and for rounding curves. Stuff well. Use hook or pencil to pack the stuffing in. It needs to be stuffed full to make the crewel stitches stand out well. Slip stitch the opening.

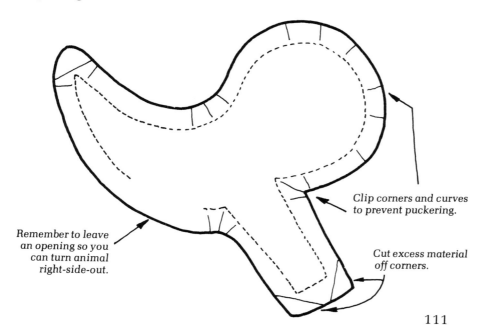

Remember to leave an opening so you can turn animal right-side-out.

Clip corners and curves to prevent puckering.

Cut excess material off corners.

111

The Projects

Scale: Each square represents 1″ square.

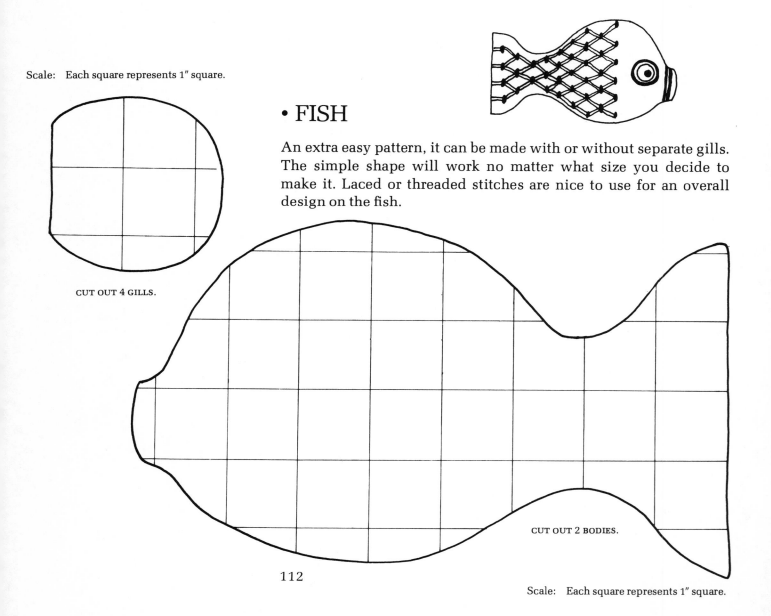

CUT OUT 4 GILLS.

• FISH

An extra easy pattern, it can be made with or without separate gills. The simple shape will work no matter what size you decide to make it. Laced or threaded stitches are nice to use for an overall design on the fish.

CUT OUT 2 BODIES.

Scale: Each square represents 1″ square.

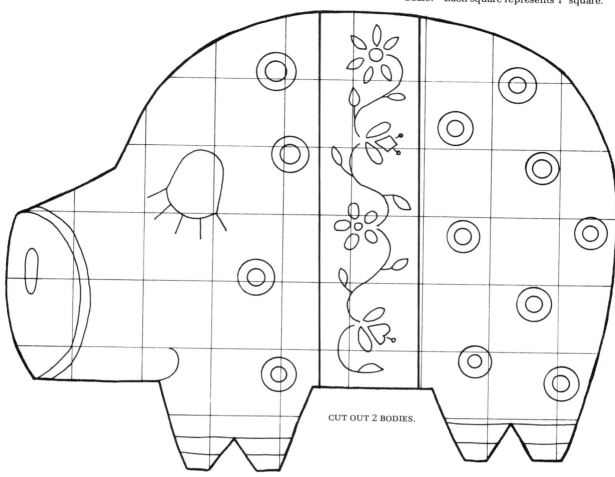

CUT OUT 2 BODIES.

• PIG

The pig is an easy pattern which works up very nicely. It can be made to any size. With fabric or felt ears and a yarn tail, the pieces go together easily. If you think of all the designs you've seen on piggy banks, you'll be well on your way to coming up with a good idea for decorating the pig.

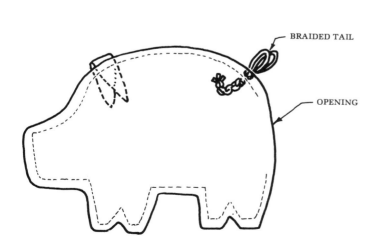

BRAIDED TAIL

OPENING

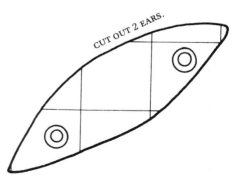

CUT OUT 2 EARS.

Scale: Each square represents 1″ square.

YARN TASSEL

WITH OR WITHOUT WINGS

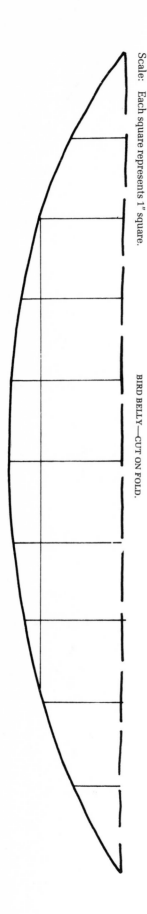

Scale: Each square represents 1" square.

BIRD BELLY—CUT ON FOLD.

• BIRD

The bird is another basic pattern. It has a gusset (the belly) added to make it stand up. You can add separate wings or draw the wings on the side of the bird. Decorate it any way you like. Background areas and outlined designs can be left plain or filled in with satin stitches or long and short stitches.

A group of birds or a combination of bird, fish and pig would make an effective mobile. You could leave out the gusset on the bird if you want to use it in a mobile.

CUT OUT 4 WINGS.

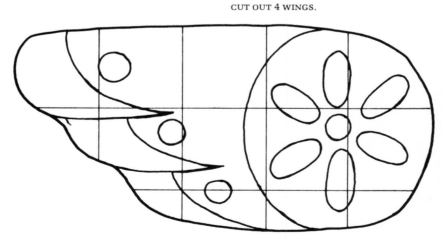

Scale: Each square represents 1" square.

114

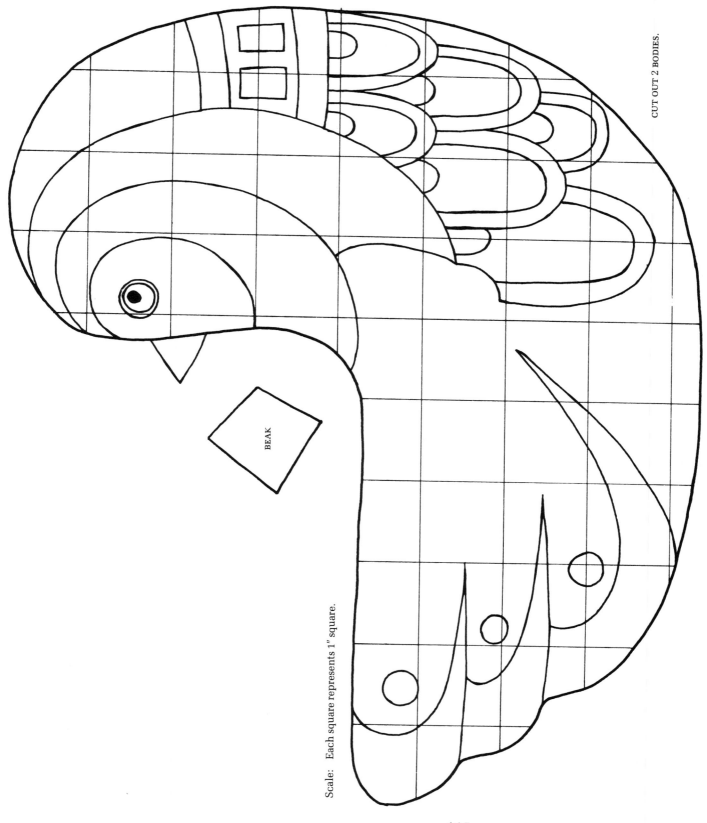

CUT OUT 2 BODIES.

BEAK

Scale: Each square represents 1" square.

• PONY/GIRAFFE

The pony/giraffe pattern is not hard to follow. Illustration above shows what a felt mane should look like on the giraffe. For the pony's mane, wrap yarn around a strip of paper. Stitch along one edge of the paper to hold the yarn together. Rip out the paper and sew the mane in place. Make a tassel or braid of yarn or felt strips for the tail, depending on what animal you are making.

Consider making the giraffe out of polka-dot fabric. If the pony were done in a striped fabric, you'd have a ready-made zebra.

The pattern has several delightful variations.

To make a rocking horse, simply add a rocker pattern.

116

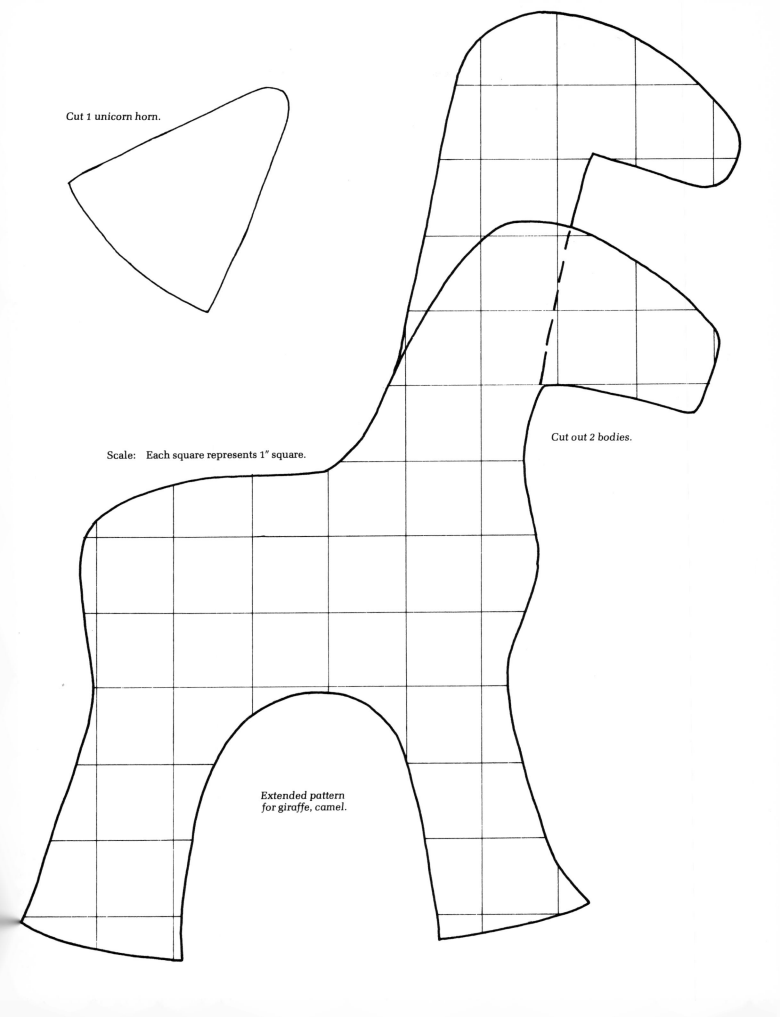

Cut 1 unicorn horn.

Scale: Each square represents 1″ square.

Cut out 2 bodies.

Extended pattern
for giraffe, camel.

Design a crewel *Pegasus*, the flying horse, by adding wings from the bird pattern.

Add a horn to the center of the pony's head to make a unicorn, the mythical, horse-like animal often shown with a goat's beard and a lion's tail.

You might come up with some other ideas, too, like changing the giraffe into a camel by adding a hump.

Cut out 4 ears.

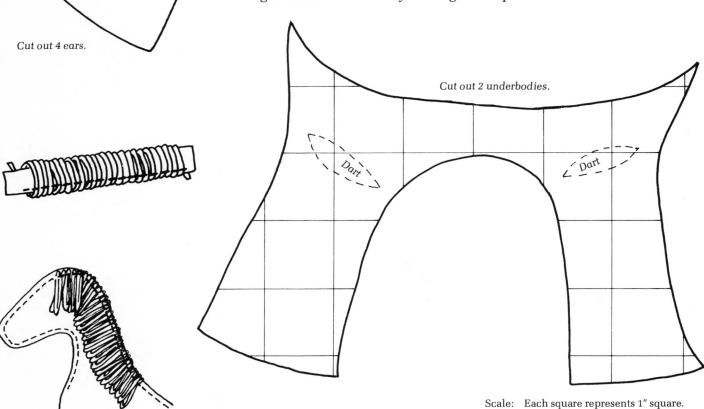

Cut out 2 underbodies.

Dart   Dart

Scale: Each square represents 1″ square.

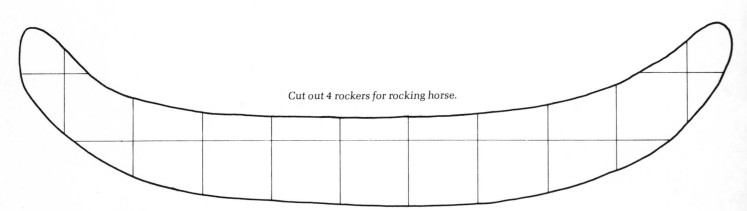

Cut out 4 rockers for rocking horse.

Scale: Each square represents 1″ square.

• HIPPO

The hippo pattern is based on a ceramic figure of a hippopotamus found in an Egyptian tomb. The original may be seen at the Metropolitan Museum of Art in New York City. The flowers on the hippo are lotus blossoms. The lotus is a tropical water lily. In Greek legend, those who ate the lotus fruit became dreamy, forgetful and lazy, living a life of ease. I don't know whether the Egyptians and the Greeks agreed but it isn't hard to imagine a lazy hippo climbing out of the Nile covered with lotus blossoms.

MATERIALS

½ yd. of a loose-weave aqua fabric; linen is recommended
30 yds. of tapestry wool or crewel wool in a dark blue green which goes well with the aqua fabric
2¾″ self-cover buttons

Transfer the pattern to the fabric. Sew all the lines in stem stitch. Do the short lines in straight stitch and the dots in French knots or straight stitch.

Press the fabric. Cut out the pattern pieces. A seam allowance of ⅜″ has already been included in the pattern.

Stitch head gusset, body gusset and underbelly to one body piece. Stitch on other body piece. Do not sew the gussets together

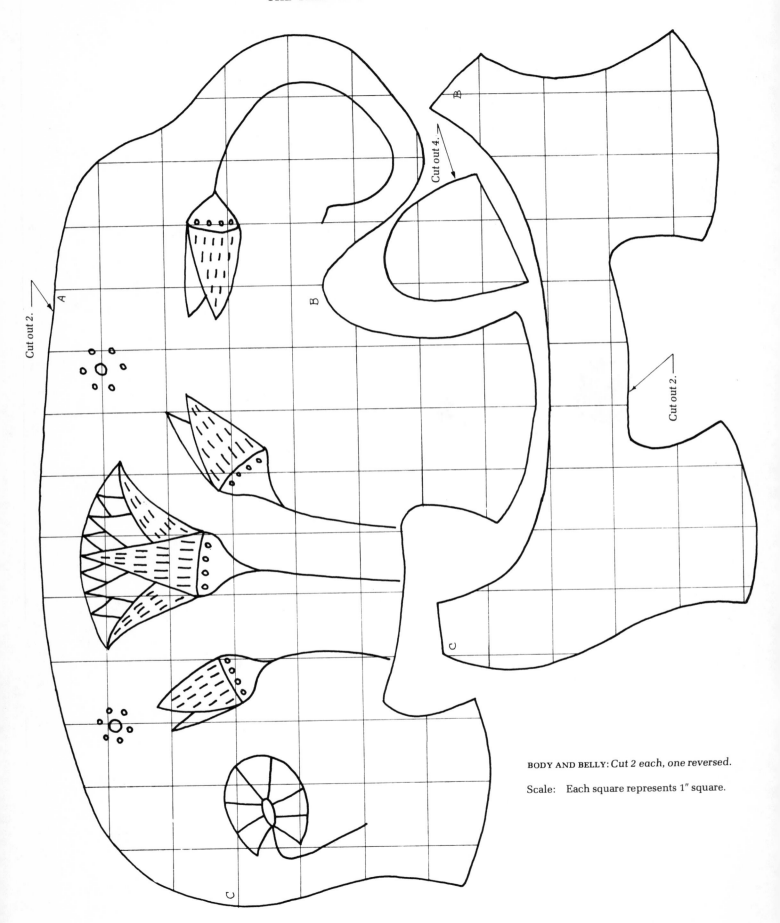

Cut out 2.

A

B

Cut out 4.

B

Cut out 2.

C

C

BODY AND BELLY: *Cut 2 each, one reversed.*

Scale: Each square represents 1″ square.

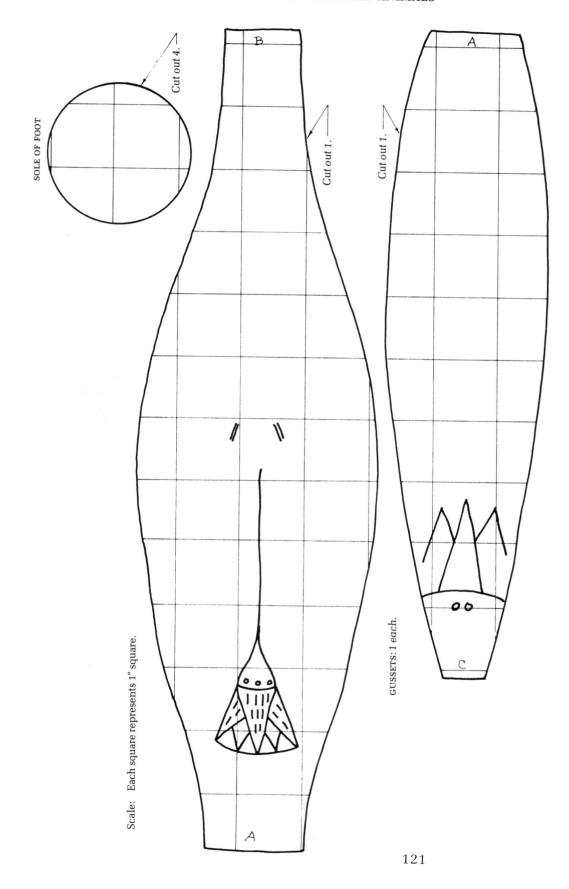

SOLE OF FOOT

Cut out 4.

Cut out 1.

Cut out 1.

GUSSETS: 1 each.

Scale: Each square represents 1" square.

B

A

A

C

121

until the animal has been stuffed. Sew the underbelly partially shut, leaving an opening so the animal can be turned right side out and stuffed.

Turn the hippo right side out and stuff, making sure the head and feet are well filled before stuffing the body. Sew gussets and underbelly opening. Run a gathering stitch around the bottoms of the feet and sew the soles of the feet in place.

Sew ear pieces together. Make a little tuck in the front of the ear and sew the open end to the head so that the back and front are separated.

Cover the self-cover buttons with aqua fabric. Stitch an eyeball in the middle or glue on a bit of black felt. Sew eyes to head around the outside edges of the button. Work the stem stitch in yarn around the eye directly over the stitches where the eye is joined to the head.

Finally, turn the hippo around and finish off the back end in stem stitch according to the illustration.

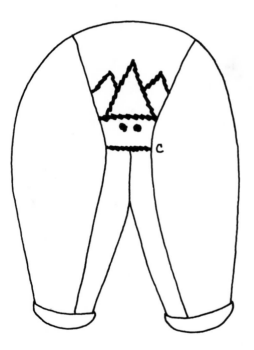
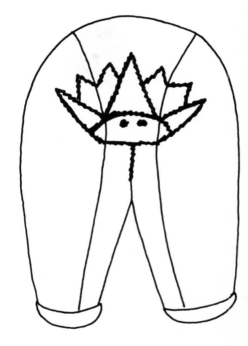

• CAT

Use the needlepoint cat pattern on pp. 145–148 and embroider it as shown opposite.

123

V

NEEDLEPOINT
ANIMALS

I used to think that doing needlepoint had to be the dullest pastime in the world until I tried it. It is easy, relaxing (when you know what you're doing), rewarding and full of endless variety. The stitches shown here are basic ones from which most others have been developed. It is easy to design your own variations, working them out on graph paper, or check other books on needlepoint for different ideas. The choice of canvas and availability of colorful yarns grows constantly. You can work on canvas so fine that it takes 784 stitches to cover 1 square inch (petit point) or on canvas so heavy that it takes only 9 stitches (or 3 stitches using a bargello stitch) to cover a square inch (quickpoint). Needlepoint is very durable. If the quality of yarn is good and if the stitches aren't so long that they snag, the work will last forever.

The term needlepoint is used here to cover all needlework done on mesh canvas. Needlepoint can be broken down into several categories: quickpoint, gros point, needlepoint and petit point, depending on how many squares are in each inch of canvas. Needlepoint can also be broken down into two stitch categories. A needlepoint stitch usually refers to a diagonal stitch crossing between adjacent squares on the canvas. A bargello stitch is a horizontal, vertical or diagonal stitch connecting squares which are usually not right next to each other.

A general rule is that the longer the stitches, the sooner the project will be finished and the shorter the stitches, the better it will wear. Keeping that in mind and with the Needlepoint Gauge Chart (p. 131) for reference, you are free to create anything you want with yarn and canvas.

Materials

• SELECTING YARNS

FOR NEEDLEPOINT: Persian and tapestry yarns are best. Persian yarn is made of 3 strands twisted together. The strands come apart easily so you can add or subtract strands for different mesh canvases. (You can also mix different color strands together.) Persian yarn comes in a wide range of colors and can be bought by the strand or by the ounce. Tapestry yarn is 4-ply but it is lighter than Persian yarn and it is hard to separate into strands. Crewel wool and knitting worsted can also be used. If you can only find the color you want in knitting worsted, use it. Knitting worsted does not wear as well as the others but it has the advantage of being the least expensive.

FOR QUICKPOINT: Quickpoint yarns are best. Good quality rug yarns work well also. If cost or color are factors, consider using knitting worsted and synthetic rug yarns.

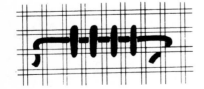

BUY YARN THAT COVERS THE CANVAS: If the canvas shows through the needlepoint, it will ruin the appearance of the work. Ecru color canvas shows through less than white canvas. If the canvas does show, use a heavier yarn. If you are working with Persian yarn, add an extra strand. If you are using a type of yarn which does not separate easily into strands, try doubling the yarn. Either it will work or the yarn will be too thick and will spread the canvas out of shape. Forcing yarn that is too thick through small mesh will shred the yarn and ruin its appearance. One possible solution is to lay strips of the yarn across the row as padding and work the stitches over the strips. If you can't find a way to make the yarn work, look for another yarn that does work or try a different mesh canvas.

ESTIMATING HOW MUCH YARN TO BUY: Work a 1″ square (3″ with sizes 3 to 5 mesh) with the same weight yarn you plan to use on the canvas you are going to use. Measure how much yarn it took. Figure the number of square inches of each color needed and multiply each by the number of yards of yarn used to cover the square inch of canvas. To find out how many skeins to buy, divide the number of yards needed by the number of yards in a skein. Different yarns are sold in different size skeins. If you are still not sure about how much you'll need, ask someone at your needlepoint store for help. Remember that it is better to buy more yarn than you think you need just to be safe. Many yarn shops will take back unused yarn. I'll bet they do that because it is so hard to figure yarn yardage.

For #10 canvas you'll need approximately 1½ yards of Persian yarn per square inch or 3 yards of tapestry yarn per square inch; #3½ canvas uses approximately ½ yard of quickpoint yarn or rug yarn per square inch.

MARKING PENS

Used for transferring the design or grid to canvas, the pen *must be waterproof.* Otherwise the ink will run when you have the article cleaned and it will bleed through the yarn. Needlepoint and art supply stores carry waterproof pens. Some pens even come in different colors if you want to mark your design by color. If you can find a gray or medium-tone waterproof marker, use that instead of black. Black may show through light color stitches. Also check the point size on the marker. You'll probably want a fine point, rather than a wide point, for better detail.

SCISSORS

You'll need a small, sharp-pointed pair for cutting single strands of yarn and a heavy pair for cutting skeins of yarn and canvas. The easiest way to cut a skein of yarn for needlepoint is to open it up into a loop and cut the loop once. Then you'll have a whole stack of strands ready to sew. Remember that it is better to work with shorter lengths of yarn (even though that means you'll have to thread your needle more often) because pieces over 18″ long will start to fray after being pulled through the canvas too many times.

CANVAS

Needlepoint canvases come in widths from 18″ to 60″. Rug canvases come in widths from 14″ to 80″. Canvases come in mesh sizes ranging from 3 (3 squares per inch) to 28 (28 squares per inch). Canvas comes in white, ecru, beige and putty colors.

MONO

MONO/SINGLE MESH/SINGLE THREAD CANVAS: Mono canvas looks like a sheet of graph paper—2 threads cross at each intersection of the mono canvas grid. It is easy to count stitches on this canvas and it works up quickly. Because only 2 threads cross at each intersection, the threads at the edge of the canvas tend to pull apart. It is important to tape or glue the edges to prevent raveling. A heavier weight yarn is sometimes needed to cover the canvas because each stitch has only a single supporting point behind it. Mono canvas comes in many mesh sizes. It is white.

PENELOPE

PENELOPE/DOUBLE MESH/DOUBLE THREADED CANVAS: One advantage to this canvas is that it provides two separate supporting points behind each stitch. A lighter weight yarn can be used on penelope than on mono. The edges are less apt to fray, though they should be taped anyway. If you want more detail, you can stitch between the double strands and get twice as many stitches in the same space. This is called "splitting the double thread." Because of the double strands, the hole you stick the needle through is smaller, and it is harder to count and keep track of where you are if you are a beginner. Penelope comes in many mesh sizes. It is made in ecru (natural) and white.

OTHER FABRICS: Other fabrics which can be used instead of canvas are monk's cloth, hardanger cloth, heavy linen and burlap.

NEEDLES

Select a blunt needle with an eye large enough to thread with the yarn you want to use. Needles are sized by numbers. See the Needlepoint Chart (p. 131). They are called tapestry needles, darning needles, yarn needles, quickpoint needles and rug needles, depending on the size you want. There are also plastic yarn needles the same size as quickpoint needles.

WHITE GLUE

Heavy-duty white glue or fabric glue is needed for sealing all the edges of the animal so they won't ravel when you sew the pieces together.

STUFFING

Use a fiberfill or polyfill stuffing for needlepoint. Foam stuffings will stick to the yarn and come through the stitches and make a mess. If you want to use foam, make a muslin pillow from the animal pattern. Stuff it with foam chips and then sew the pillow inside the needlepoint shell.

BACKING FABRIC

If you only want to do the front side of the animal in needlepoint, make the back and other pieces from another fabric. Corduroy, velvet, felt, heavy cotton, canvas or any relatively heavy fabric will do. Choose the fabric for color first, rather than type of fabric. Find a color which matches or complements the needlepoint. Normally you would choose a solid color but a floral or geometric print might make a nice change.

NEEDLEPOINT GAUGE CHART

Name	Canvas Mesh Size	Needle Size	Persian wool 3 strand. Separates.	Crewel wool 2 strand. Separates.	Cotton or silk floss. 6 strand. Separates.	Tapestry Yarn. Doesn't separate.	Quickpoint Yarn. Doesn't separate.	Knitting Worsted. Doesn't separate.	Rug Wool. Doesn't separate.
Quickpoint and Rug Canvas	3–3½	10–13					2	4	2–3
	4–5	13 (yarn, quickpoint or rug needle)	9	6		4	1–2	3–4	1–2
	6	16	6	5		3	1	3	1
	7	16	6	4		3	1	2	1
Gros Point	8	16–18	5–6	4		2		2	1
	10	17–19	3	3		1–2		1	
	12	17–19	3	3		1		1	
Needlepoint	13–14	19–20	2	2					
	16	19–22	1	2	12				
	18	20–24	1	1	10–12				
Petit Point	20–24	22–24	1	1	4–6				

Notes: Yarn quantities are given in numbers of strands; the yarns that don't separate are given in whole strands. You probably will need to use an extra strand of Persian, crewel and tapestry yarn to cover canvas when doing bargello stitches.

SPECIAL PROJECTS USING EMBROIDERY FLOSS

Since there is a growing interest in working with silk and cotton embroidery floss we are including a list of animal projects which can be done using embroidery floss. The following patterns can be made up on needlepoint canvas (#16 mesh to #20 mesh) in cotton or silk floss. Both cotton and silk floss work up about the same.

Hooked Animals: Work these up in needlepoint and bargello stitches.

Ladybug (2-D or 3-D)

Hedgehog (2-D or 3-D)

Turtle (2-D)

Panda (2-D)

Needlepoint Animals: These work up to be lovely miniatures of the originals. The sheen of the floss makes them extra special.

Snail (2-D or 3-D)

Cat (2-D or 3-D)

Owl (2-D or 3-D)

Indian Painted Elephant (2-D)

Crewel/Embroidery Animals: Of course these can be done on fabric using floss but the patterns also work beautifully on needlepoint canvas.

Pig (2-D or 3-D)

Fish (2-D or 3-D)

Bird (2-D or 3-D)

Pony/Giraffe and variations (2-D)

Note: *2-D (two dimensional)* means to make the design up flat, as a picture, pillow, design or anything which does not require the animal shape to be cut out around its edges. Size would make that difficult. *3-D (three dimensional)* means the pattern can be made up as a stuffed animal.

Floss could be used for detail on the knit and crochet finger puppets.

Tiny woolly animals could also be made using floss. The octopus, mini-monster and magnet animals made with miniature pompoms would be beautiful. Imagine them stitched to a hat or a collar for a three dimensional decoration. Or use them as stuffed animals in a doll house.

Stitches and Techniques

• STITCHES

To make the stitches, follow the numbers in the diagrams. Put your needle up through the canvas at #1 and down through the canvas at #2. Always come up through the odd numbers and go down through the even numbers.

    Continental Stitch: Use this for outlining areas and wherever a single line of stitches or a small area of stitches is needed. It covers the canvas well, wears well and has a slightly padded appearance. It uses the same amount of yarn as the basketweave stitch. Used in combination with the basketweave stitch, you need not learn many other stitches. Work this stitch from right to left, turning the canvas upside down for return rows.

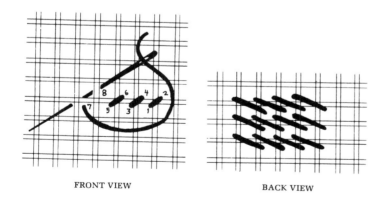

FRONT VIEW   BACK VIEW

    Basketweave/Diagonal/Tent/Diagonal Tent Stitch: This stitch has a lot of different names and looks a bit difficult at first but is very easy and fast once you learn it. Use it to fill in areas outlined by the continental stitch. It is better to use as a filler stitch than the continental because it distorts the canvas much less. It uses the same amount of yarn. The name basketweave comes from the woven appearance the stitch gives the back of the canvas. It covers well and wears well. Note the needle position. Going diagonally from right to left (up) the needle goes through the canvas horizontally. Going diagonally from left to right (down) the needle goes through the canvas vertically.

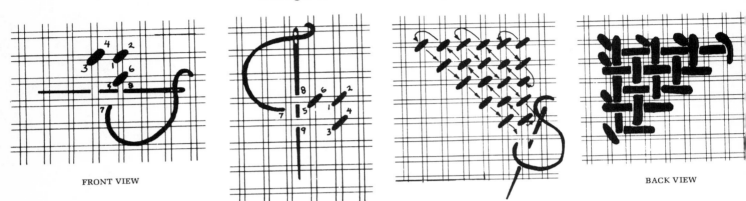

FRONT VIEW   BACK VIEW

Half Cross Stitch: This stitch uses the smallest amount of yarn but does not cover the canvas as effectively as the continental and basketweave stitches. It should be used for articles that will not receive heavy wear. Always work the half cross stitch on double mesh canvas. The stitch is worked from left to right and the canvas is turned upside down to work return rows. The needle always goes through the canvas vertically.

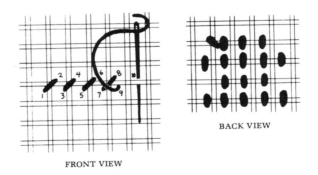

FRONT VIEW   BACK VIEW

Flame/Bargello/Florentine/Hungarian/Straight/Straight Gobelin Stitch: The vertical flame stitch creates a zigzag pattern. Many different pattern variations are possible by altering the length of

134

the stitches and the placement of the stitches according to color. Peaks and diamonds, curves and circles can be formed according to the way stitches of the same color meet. It is a simple, fast, vertical filler stitch, worked back and forth, crossing over 2, 3, 4 or more horizontal threads. It may require 1 more strand of yarn than the continental or basketweave stitch for complete coverage. Work out a guide row or shape (like the diamond outlines on the owl's chest) and then fill in the rest of the rows or shapes.

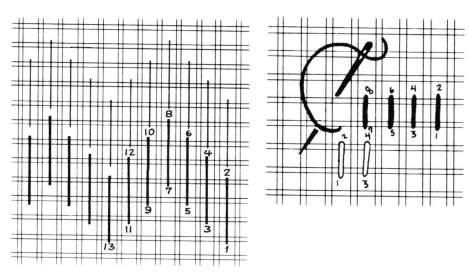

Encroaching Gobelin: This stitch is just like the straight Gobelin only it slants over 1 vertical row as it crosses 2 to 5 horizontal rows.

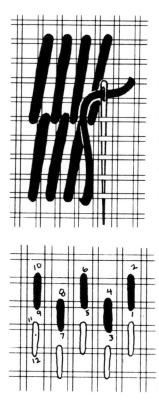

Brick Stitch: The description of the straight stitch applies here. It has less tendency to snag.

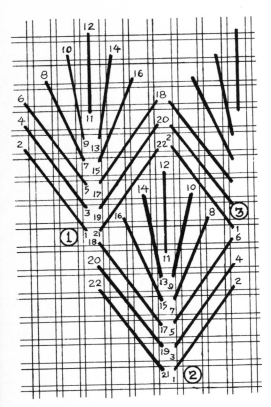

Leaf Stitch: The leaves are used upside down for feathers on the owl. The leaf can be worked from left to right (1), from right to left (2), or stopped at any point (3).

Turkey Tufting: Turkey tufting creates a looped or shaggy effect. It is exactly the same as rya done on canvas with a needle. The loops can be any length you want. They can be left as loops or cut to look furry. If you are covering several rows, work from the bottom left up, if possible, so the loops don't get tangled. Use this stitch extra long for a lion's mane or an Angora cat. Or cut it short for a rug-like texture. In the illustration, Row 1 shows the loops cut; Row 2 shows the uncut loops; Row 3 shows how to make a single tuft. You can work the continental stitch between rows of tufting so the canvas doesn't show through.

ROW 3

ROW 2

ROW 1

• TECHNIQUES

STARTING AND ENDING OFF A LENGTH OF YARN

Pull the yarn through the canvas so that a 1″ tail is left on the back of the canvas. Hold that tail against the canvas and sew around it as you make your stitches so that it is completely covered. When you get to the end of a strand of yarn, thread the yarn through the back of several stitches to anchor it, and cut off the excess.

PREPARING THE CANVAS

Cut a square or rectangle of canvas which is big enough to allow a 1″ to 2″ border all around the design.

Measure the width and length of the canvas and write the measurements down to help with blocking.

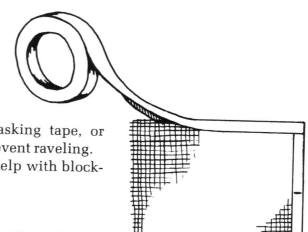

Tape over the edges of the canvas with masking tape, or drizzle a line of white glue around the outside to prevent raveling.

Mark the center of each side of the canvas to help with blocking.

TRANSFERRING THE DESIGN TO CANVAS

The designs in this book have been reduced. To make the design full size again, draw a grid of horizontal and vertical lines 1″ apart on the canvas using a waterproof marker. Then you have two choices.

METHOD 1: Copy the design freehand from the pattern onto the enlarged graph, marking points where the outline crosses the grid line and connecting the points. If you work carefully, the drawing will be very close to the original.

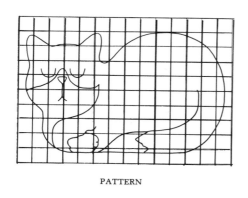

PATTERN

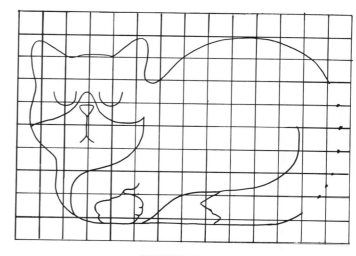

ENLARGED GRAPH

If you need a reverse of the pattern, like for the back of the elephant, copy the squares in reverse. You might want to trace the original out of the book, turn the tracing over and work from the back.

METHOD 2: It isn't necessary to transfer the drawing to the canvas. Once the graph is on the canvas you can "read" directly from the graphed pattern in the book, matching the stitches in each square of the graph.

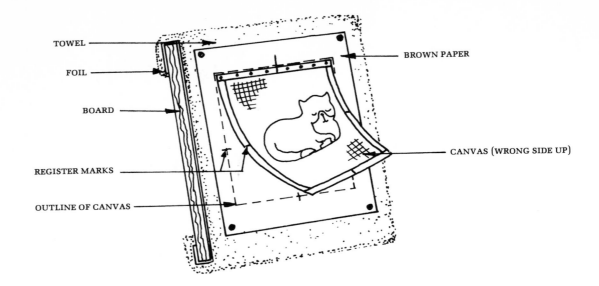

TOWEL

FOIL

BOARD

REGISTER MARKS

OUTLINE OF CANVAS

BROWN PAPER

CANVAS (WRONG SIDE UP)

BLOCKING

Blocking is necessary when the needlepoint stitches pull the canvas out of shape so that the corners are no longer square. It is quick and easy to do on the size pieces you are working with in this book.

Find a clean piece of board or plywood that is larger than the canvas to be blocked. Cover the board with aluminum foil and then with a towel.

On a piece of brown paper, draw a rectangle or square matching the original measurements of your prepared canvas. Mark the center of each side of the outline. Tack the brown paper outline on top of the towel with rustproof tacks or push pins.

Place the canvas face down on the brown paper outline. Match the register marks on the canvas as closely as possible with those on the brown paper. Tack those points down using rustproof tacks or push pins. Then tack the edges on the canvas (alternating from side to side) along the outline.

Put a damp cloth over the canvas. Iron it lightly at wool setting until the canvas is dampened. Stretch and pull the damp canvas until it matches the register marks and outline all the way around. Move the tacks when necessary. Tack the rest of the canvas down, spacing the tacks no more than an inch apart.

Let the canvas dry completely. Keep it in a horizontal position away from direct sunlight. Leave it tacked to the board for two or more days until it is completely dry. If you want to speed up the drying process, you can iron the canvas dry.

Note: The stitches can be fluffed by steaming the front side with an iron held at least 4″ above the canvas. To help protect the needlepoint, it can be sprayed with Scotchgard stain repeller according to directions on the can for upholstery fabric.

SEWING ANIMALS TOGETHER

There are 3 methods. Method 1 must be used if you want to sew a fabric backing to the animal. Methods 1 and 2 are recommended for animals like the cat, whose colors do not change very often along the edges to be joined. Method 3 is best for animals whose patterns and colors change constantly along the outside edges, like the owl. Remember, always complete the needlepoint before cutting the pieces out.

METHOD 1: Cut the animal out, leaving a 1″ border of bare canvas around the needlepoint. Glue the cut edges with white glue. Where the pattern is indented, draw a wide glue line as close to the indentation as possible. Let the glue dry thoroughly.

Cut down the middle of each glued indentation mark. Do not cut through the glue to the needlepoint. If you do, re-glue that area immediately. Then fold the canvas under and hem it to the inside of the animal. (A running stitch will work well.)

Whipstitch or feather stitch * the edges together right side out, using yarn. Change the color of the yarn to match the part of the animal you are sewing.

Leave a 4″ opening along one edge and stuff with polyfill. Whipstitch the opening.

METHOD 2: Cut the animal out as close to the needlepoint as possible. Glue the cut edges immediately with white glue. (Or glue along the edge of the needlepoint and then cut out.)

Whipstitch or feather stitch * the animal together right side out with yarn, changing colors to match the body. Stuff and close up.

METHOD 3: Cut out the animal pattern, leaving a 1″ border of bare canvas all around the needlepoint. Glue the edges with white glue.

Stitch the animal together inside out, using yarn or buttonhole thread. Leave an opening large enough to turn the animal right side out.

Turn the animal right side out. Stuff and close.

139

If you want, you can whipstitch, feather stitch,* or match the stitch pattern around the joined edges, changing the yarn to match each different color.

Note: Spray the animal with Scotchgard stain repeller to keep it clean.

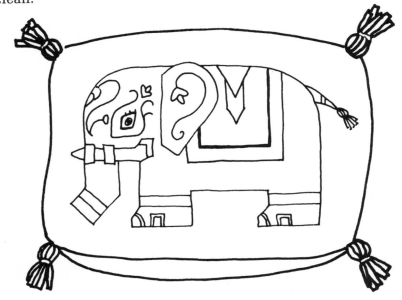

PILLOWS AND WALL HANGINGS

Any of the three-dimensional needlepoint animal patterns can be stitched as a wall hanging or a pillow. Cut the canvas to the size you want, allowing a good 2″ border all around for hemming, and transfer the animal pattern to it. Sew the background in a contrasting color.

When turning a pattern that has extra parts (like the elephant's ears and tail) into a two-dimensional design, trace those parts flat in the proper positions. Don't worry if they cover part of the body pattern. Check the illustrations to see how the extra parts have been added.

*Crewel stitch; see illustrations in Crewel, section IV.

TO MAKE DIFFERENT SIZED ANIMALS

It is very simple to make an animal in a size different from that in the instructions. Buy the size canvas you wish to work on and make the drawing of the animal larger or smaller accordingly. Check the chart above to find out what kind of yarn to use and figure out how much you will need. All of these patterns can be made on any size canvas, from petit point to rug canvas.

Note: Animal patterns in the Hooking and Rya section can be done in needlepoint. Design a back or bottom side for the two-dimensional animals if you want them to be three-dimensional.

The Projects

NEEDLEPOINT SNAIL

Snails are usually slow but this one isn't. It's an easy pattern that's fun to do because it has lots of colors to mix up any way you want.

MATERIALS

Scraps of knitting worsted in as many colors as you want
#10 mono canvas, 12" x 24"
Strip of fabric for base, 3" x 10"
Stuffing

Tape over the edges of the canvas with masking tape or drizzle a line of white glue around the outside to prevent raveling.

Use Method 1 for Transferring the design to canvas.

Do eyes and mouth in continental stitch. Do the continental stitch in black along the outlines on the shell. Fill in the background areas in your choice of colors. Use one of the following stitches: continental, basketweave or straight.

Cut out the pieces along the outside edge of the glue line. Cut the base piece from the fabric.

Starting from the tail, sew the base to the body pieces inside out. Turn the snail right side out and whipstitch (see illustration 2, p. 203), or feather stitch (see p. 105) the edges together in body color for the body and in black for the shell section. Stuff, then sew it shut.

Make 2 or 4 tight little braids for antennae; sew on so they seem to be coming out of the top of the snail's head. (See illustration.)

Variations

Design your own simple shapes—illustrations show ideas to get you started.

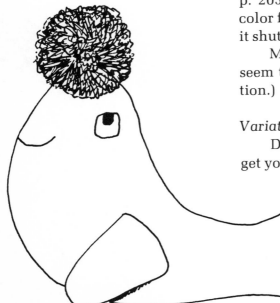

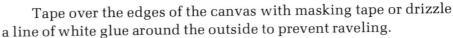

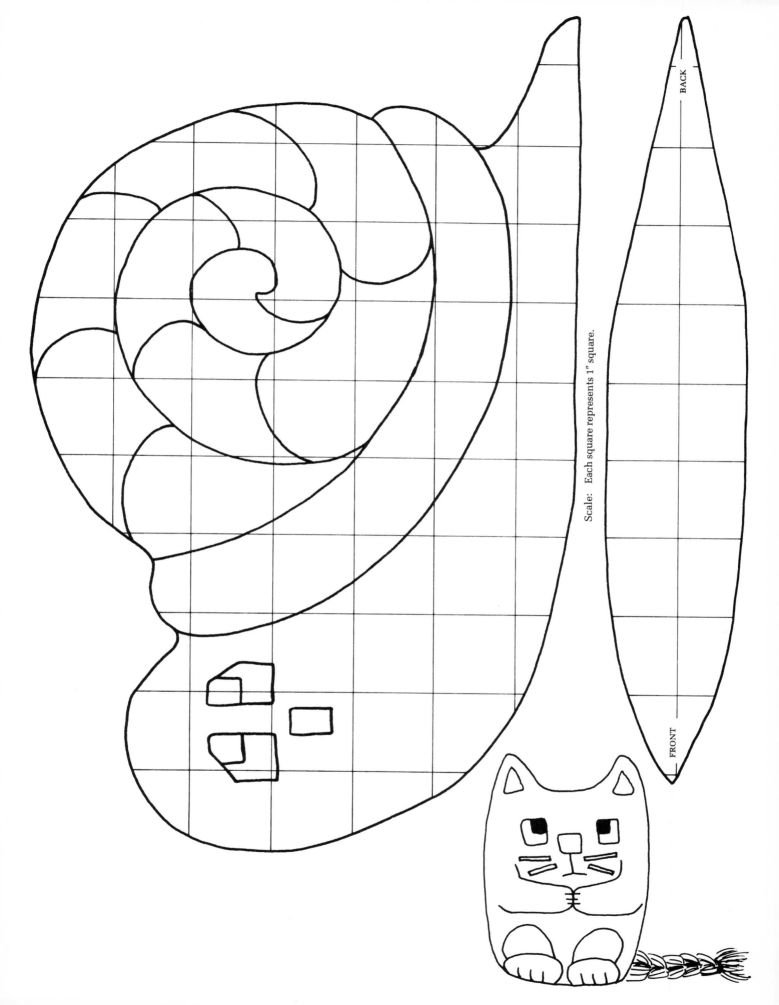

Scale: Each square represents 1" square.

BACK

FRONT

• NEEDLEPOINT CAT

If you're a cat lover, this is for you. Check all the stitch possibilities suggested in the instructions and look through all the related illustrations. If you don't find one that looks like your cat, work out your own design. With this simple pattern, it isn't hard at all.

MATERIALS

    Persian wool: 160 yds. main color (gray)

                 80 yds. second color (off-white)

                 3 yds. nose color (pink)

                 6 yds. black

    #10 Mono canvas: 2 pieces, 17" x 13"

                 1 piece, 17" x 7", or substitute matching piece(s) of fabric for the canvas if you don't want to do the back and/or bottom of the cat in needlepoint.

    Polyfill stuffing

    Yarn needle

Cut the canvas to the correct size and follow instructions for preparing the canvas.

Follow Method 1 or 2 for transferring the design to canvas.

To work the cat design, first do the single lines of stitching using the continental stitch. Then fill in the large areas. If you use the straight stitch or the brick stitch, crossing over 4 threads on the canvas, the cat will work up very quickly and won't need to be blocked. Or you can use the basketweave stitch or the continental stitch and block the pieces.

Follow instructions for blocking, if necessary.

Use Method 1 or 2 for sewing animal together.

Note: If you feel like experimenting, look at the illustrations of other designs based on the cat. The cat can also be done on quickpoint or rug canvas. If you make it in the same dimensions given in the instructions, it will be done very quickly. It takes about 6 ounces of rug yarn on #4 canvas. Try working the cat in a larger size. Or consider blowing the pattern up and using the lion or tiger suggestions (p. 148).

(More detailed graphs pages 146–8.)

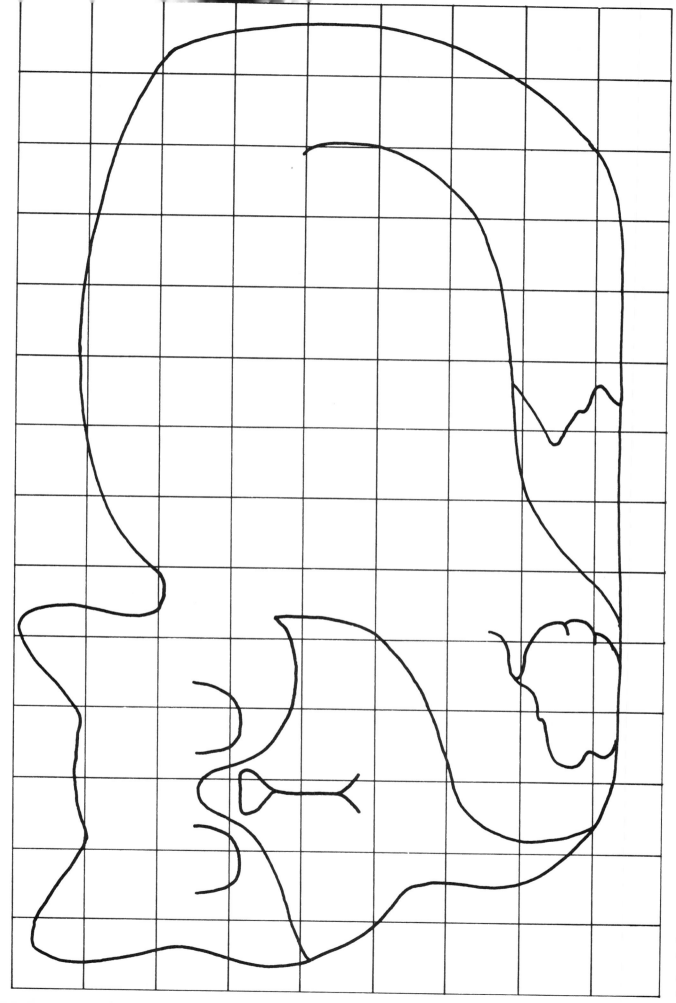

FRONT VIEW OF CAT

Scale: Each square represents 1" square.

If you're transferring by Method 1, use these patterns for a color guide. If you're using Method 2, you can read colors directly from these graphs.

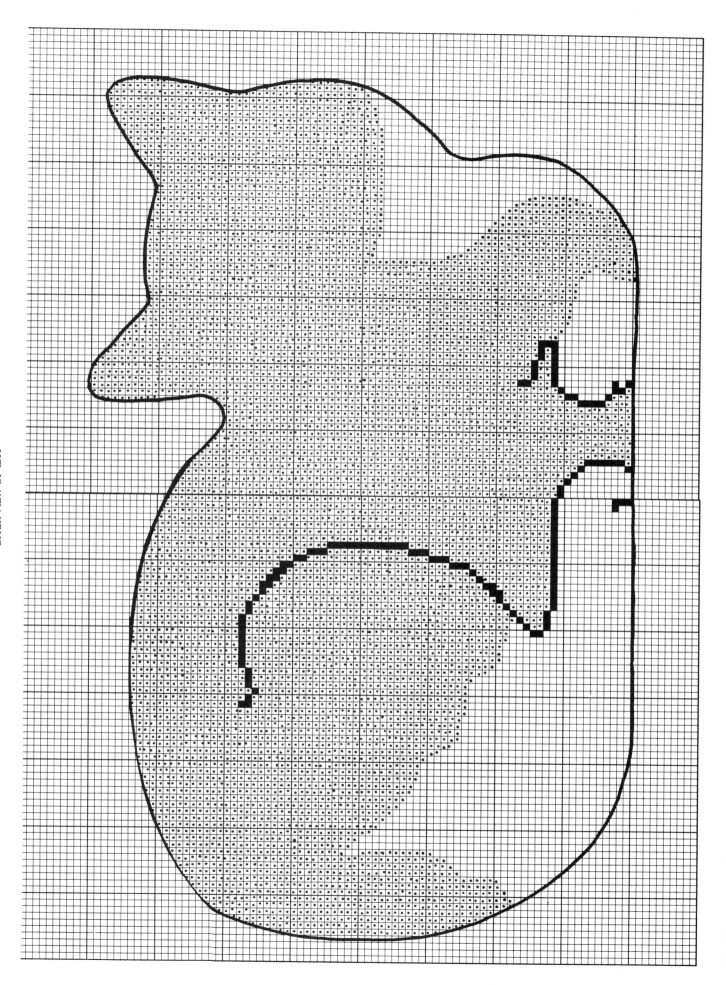

BACK VIEW OF CAT

BOTTOM VIEW OF CAT   Could be made out of felt.

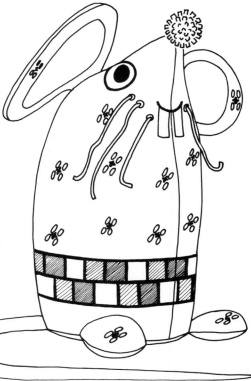

• NEEDLEPOINT MOUSE

This is a more detailed pattern than the other needlepoint projects, but the result is worth it. The mouse stands one foot tall. Because it's done on #5 canvas, the needlepoint goes quickly.

If you love the mouse but would rather not get involved with so much needlepoint, the pattern works just as well on fabric with the details done in crewel.

However you decide to make the mouse, I'm sure you'll love the finished product.

MATERIALS

    Quickpoint yarn: 1 yd. white
                     1 oz. yellow (honey gold) (⁹⁄₁₀ oz. okay)
                     1¼ oz. orange (tangerine)
                     12 oz. light green (lime green)
                     1 oz. dark green (fern green) (⁹⁄₁₀ oz. okay)
    #5 Double mesh canvas: 2′ x 3′
    Heavy fabric for base of body, soles of feet and tail: 1′ x 2′
    Polyester stuffing
    Yarn needle
    Design

Tape edges of canvas.

Transfer design to canvas.

Use continental stitch to do eyes, mouth, scattered flowers and outline of border around lower part of mouse. Then fill in the background using one of the following: basketweave, continental, straight or brick stitch.

Block if necessary.

Cut out pieces and follow Method 2 for sewing needlepoint animals together.

Make a 1½″-diameter pompom nose in orange. Make whiskers by pulling 10″ strands of yarn through the nose area. Knot on both sides of nose to keep them in place. (See illustration.) And don't forget to make a fabric or braided tail. (See illustration.)

149

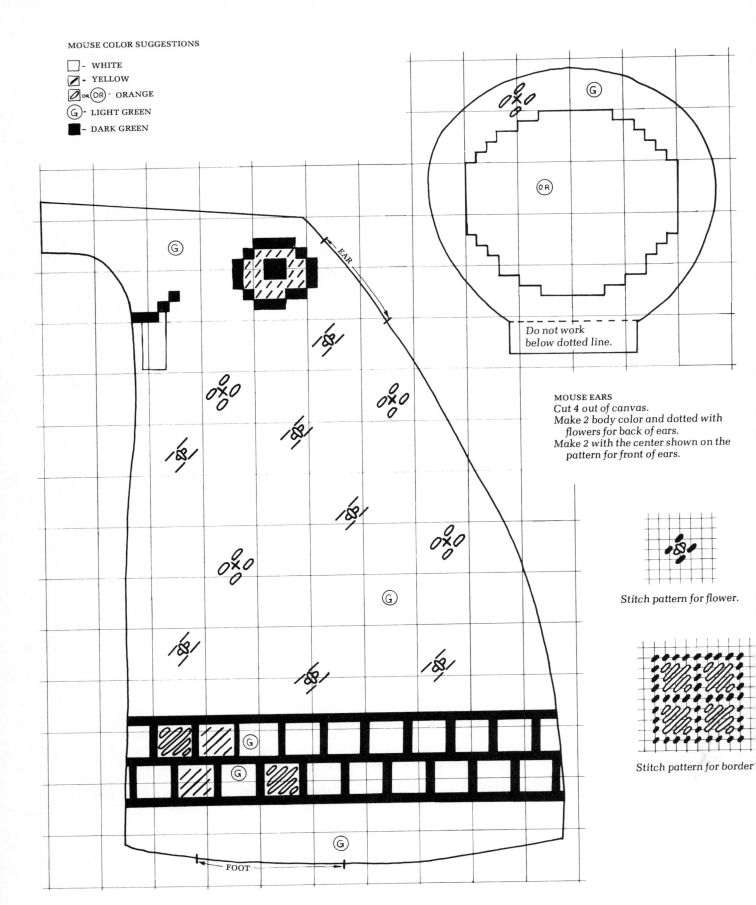

MOUSE COLOR SUGGESTIONS

- WHITE
- YELLOW
- OR - ORANGE
- G - LIGHT GREEN
- DARK GREEN

Do not work
below dotted line.

MOUSE EARS
Cut 4 out of canvas.
Make 2 body color and dotted with
    flowers for back of ears.
Make 2 with the center shown on the
    pattern for front of ears.

Stitch pattern for flower.

Stitch pattern for border.

EAR

FOOT

MOUSE SIDE
Cut 2 out of canvas.

Scale: Each square represents 1″ square.

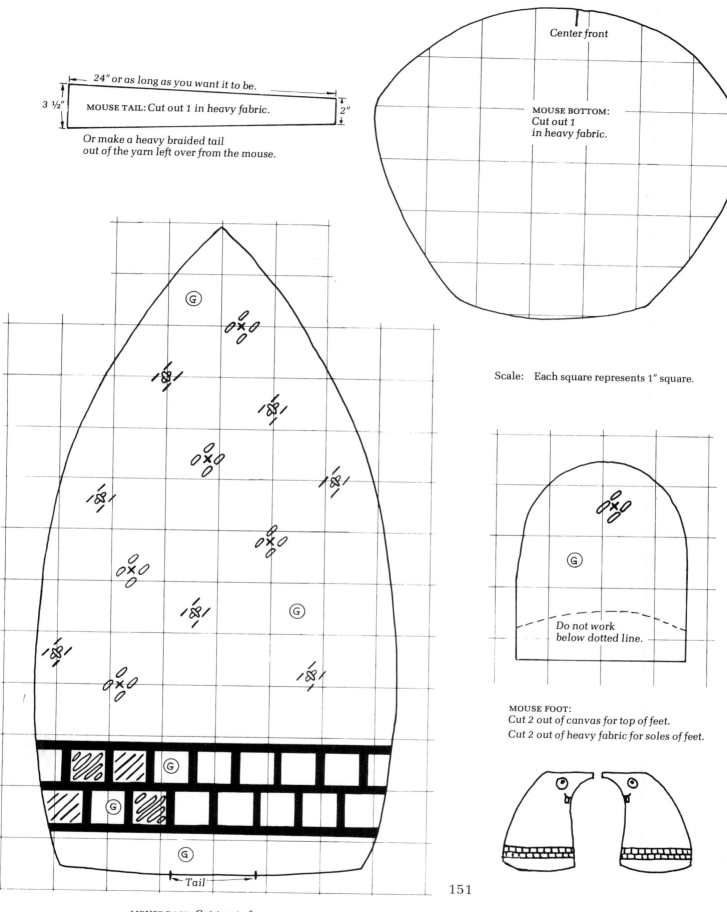

24" or as long as you want it to be.

3 ½"

MOUSE TAIL: Cut out 1 in heavy fabric.

2"

Or make a heavy braided tail
out of the yarn left over from the mouse.

Center front

MOUSE BOTTOM:
Cut out 1
in heavy fabric.

Scale: Each square represents 1" square.

G

Do not work
below dotted line.

MOUSE FOOT:
Cut 2 out of canvas for top of feet.
Cut 2 out of heavy fabric for soles of feet.

G

G

G

Tail

151

MOUSE BACK: Cut 1 out of canvas.

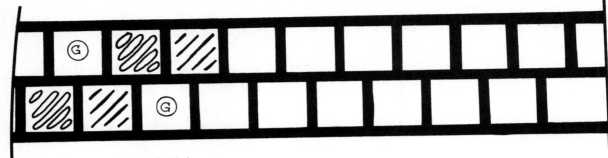

Border for right front half of mouse.

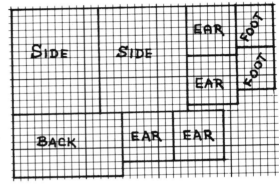

How to lay out mouse pattern on 2' x 3' canvas.

Variation

RABBIT: Work same as mouse but use rabbit ears and make a large pompom tail.

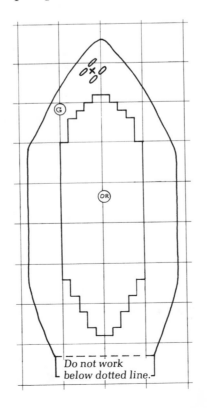

Do not work below dotted line.

RABBIT EAR
Cut 4 out of canvas.
Make 2 body color
for back of ears.
Make 2 with the center
shown on the pattern for front of ears.

• NEEDLEPOINT OWL

Besides being a charming fellow, our owl is a needlepoint sampler. He combines several different bargello and needlepoint stitches.

MATERIALS
    Persian wool: 2 yds. white
                35 yds. off-white (or 37 yds. white)
                2 yds. gold
                1 yd. dark gold (or 3 yds. gold)
                2 yds. black
                60 yds. beige
                60 yds. light brown
                60 yds. brown
                60 yds. dark brown
    #10 Mono canvas: 2 pieces, 10″ x 13″ (or substitute a matching piece of fabric for one of the pieces of canvas if you don't want to do the back of the bird in needlepoint.
    Polyfill stuffing
    Yarn needle
    Coat hanger (thin wire)
    Scraps of black or brown felt
    White glue
    Wire cutters
    Pliers

Cut the canvas to the correct size and follow instructions for preparing the canvas.

Follow Method 1 for transferring the design to canvas.

To draw the back view of the owl, trace the outside line of the owl and the line dividing the body and the legs onto the canvas.

To work the owl design, first do the features of the face using the continental stitch. Then fill in the background area of the face using the basketweave or continental stitch. Next follow the dark outline of the pattern on the chest using the straight stitch. Fill in the outline, following the color pattern on the drawing, using the straight stitch. Do the feathers (see leaf stitch, p. 136) in rows, working from the bottom to the top. The colors and placement of rows are indicated on the drawing. Finally do the legs. Fill them in using either the continental stitch or the feather stitch.

Fill in the back of the owl in feather stitch rows matching the front colors and finish the legs the way you did them on the front.

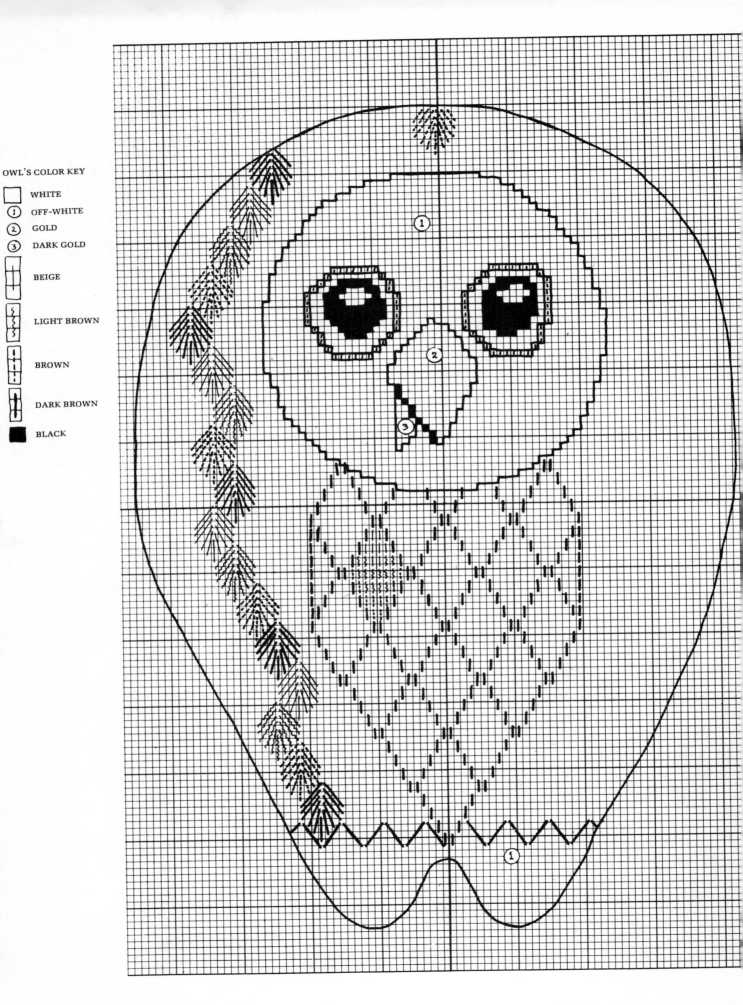

OWL'S COLOR KEY

WHITE
① OFF-WHITE
② GOLD
③ DARK GOLD
BEIGE
LIGHT BROWN
BROWN
DARK BROWN
BLACK

This pattern probably won't need blocking but if it does, follow the instructions for blocking.

For the owl's feet, cut the bottom of a thin wire coat hanger in half. With a pair of pliers, bend each end of the wire into a claw shape. Cut 2 felt leg covers and 2 felt tops and bottoms for the owl's feet. Glue the leg covers around the lower part of the legs. Let them dry and trim off the excess felt along the sides. Then glue the felt feet together around the wire claws. Let them dry and then trim away the excess felt around the wire. Be careful not to cut through to the wire.

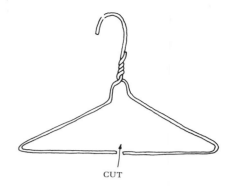

CUT

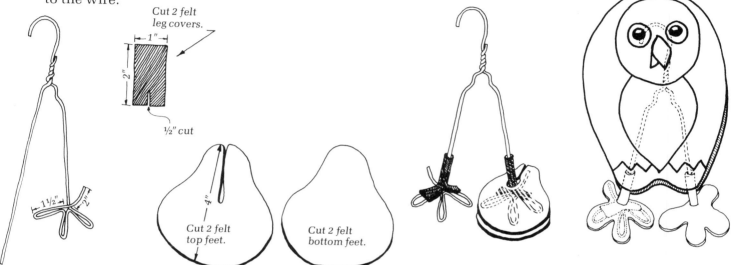

Cut 2 felt leg covers.

1"

2"

1/2" cut

Cut 2 felt top feet.

4"

Cut 2 felt bottom feet.

1 1/2"

2"

Follow Method 3 for sewing needlepoint animals together. Sew the owl together inside out until you get to the legs. Then turn the owl right side out. Stick the coat hanger inside, stuff the owl and finish sewing the legs together from the outside.

Variations

See illustrations below.

Note: If you design your own bird, make the feet big enough to support it. If the bird is larger than the owl, make the claws at least 2" long and make larger felt foot covers.

155

• NEEDLEPOINT ELEPHANT

Here is an elegant Indian elephant for the person who enjoys detailed needlepoint. You can work both sides in needlepoint or do one side in needlepoint and substitute a nice backing fabric for the other side.

MATERIALS

> *Persian wool:* 6 yds. white
> 10 yds. green
> 10 yds. rose
> 12 yds. magenta
> 10 yds. dark gold
> 15 yds. light gold
> 6 yds. black
> 90 yds. gray

Note: You can substitute any colors. Check the General Chart if you plan to use a different type of yarn. If you want to use tapestry yarn, you'll need twice as much.

> *#10 Mono canvas:* 2 pieces, 11″ x 15″ (or 1 piece of canvas and a piece of heavy backing fabric.) (You can also use Penelope canvas and you can work in a size other than #10.)
> Polyfill or cotton batting
> Yarn needle

Cut the canvas to the correct size and follow instructions for preparing the canvas.

Follow Method 2 for transferring the design to canvas. The heavy black outlines on the pattern are there as a guide in case you want to draw the elephant on canvas or use the pattern for a crewel or hooking project.

This project can be completed in the continental and basket-weave stitches. It can also be done, much more quickly, using the brick stitch (crossing over 5 threads) for the background and longer Gobelin stitches, either horizontally or vertically, wherever the stitch covers more than one row. Use the continental or Gobelin stitch for single lines in the design. You can also design any kind of stitches you want to fill in the different areas. Don't feel constricted by the pattern. Experiment. The elephant looks very good with more shading detail, too.

ELEPHANT COLOR CODE

☐	GRAY
☑	WHITE
■	BLACK
◩	LIGHT GOLD
☒	DARK GOLD
⊡	GREEN
⊞	AQUA
◪	ROSE

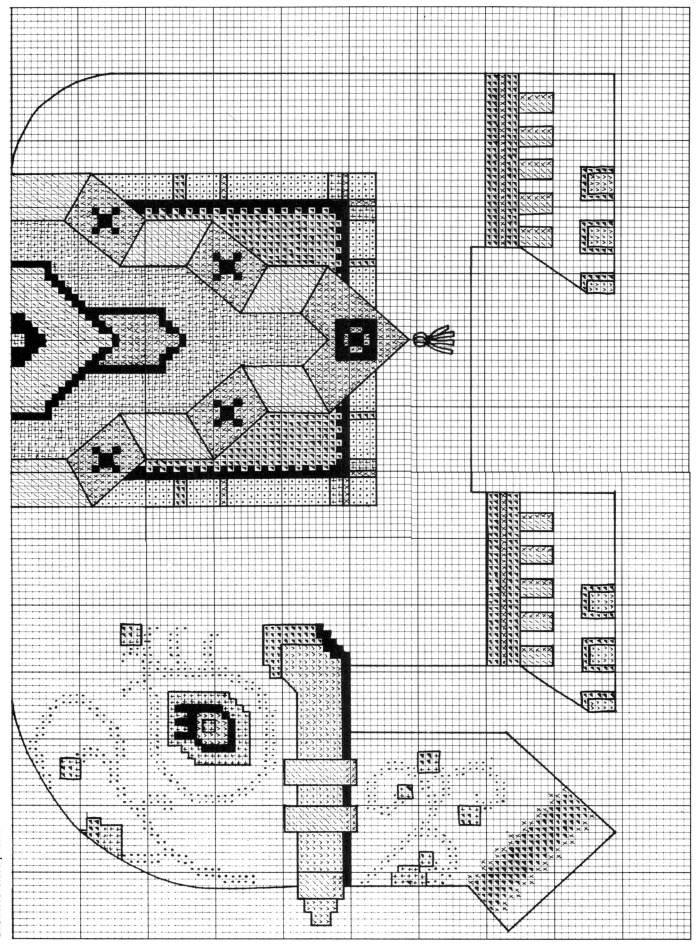

Shown reversed p. 158.

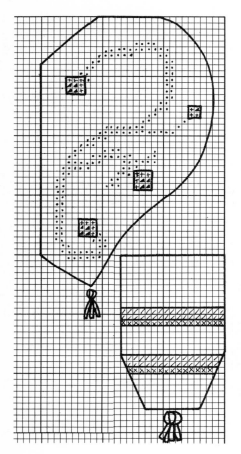

If you use the continental stitch and basketweave stitch, you may need to follow the instructions for blocking.

Finish by following Method 1 for sewing needlepoint animals together. Attach ears before sewing the body together. Do not over-stuff.

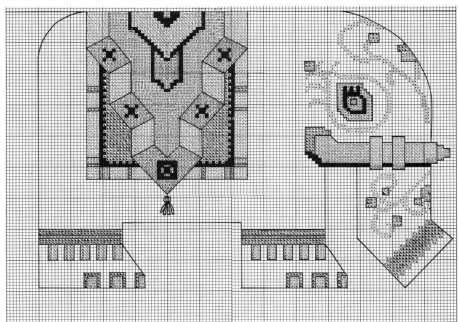

ELEPHANT
COLOR CODE

☐	GRAY
V	WHITE
■	BLACK
╱	LIGHT GOLD
X	DARK GOLD
•	GREEN
+	AQUA
◢	ROSE

158

VI

KNITTED ANIMALS

Knitting means to make a net by making loops and pulling loops through loops, usually with two pointed sticks. Archaeologists say that it was a skill developed by early man to make webs and nets out of roots and vines. It's easy to do. There are only two basic stitches to learn. Knitted items have more elasticity than crocheted items. It is not as easy to create unusual shapes in knitting as it is in crocheting because you are limited to working back and forth in rows or around in tubes. But that doesn't take the fun out of it. All kinds of interesting patterns can be knitted. There are many books available which tell you how to knit borders, designs and overall patterns (stripes, checks, plaids, diamonds, flowers, etc.). You might use some of the simple animal shapes here to practice intricate knit designs. I find knitting more relaxing than crocheting because there seems to be less to keep track of when you're knitting.

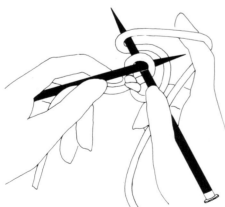

General Directions

• KNITTING NEEDLES

STRAIGHT KNITTING NEEDLES: Straight needles are used for knitting back and forth in rows. They are used in pairs. One end is pointed and the other end has a disc to keep the stitches from sliding off. They are made in aluminum, plastic, wood or steel and come in lengths ranging from 10″ to 16″. The 10″ needles are a good size for the projects in this book.

CIRCULAR KNITTING NEEDLES: Knitting around and around to form a tube shape is done on a single round needle. The needle, from 11″ to 29″ long, has points at both ends and can hold a large number of stitches. When you do the stockinette stitch on a circular needle you knit every row instead of having to knit one row and purl the next. If you want to try out a circular needle, try making a long, striped snake.

DOUBLE-POINTED NEEDLES: Double-pointed needles, made of aluminum, steel or plastic, are used in sets of 4 or 5. They are good for working on smaller tube shapes like socks and mittens. When you do the stockinette stitch on double-pointed needles, you knit every row, as on circular needles. Try them out on the elephant or any animal puppet patterns.

SELECTING NEEDLES: Use fat needles for bulky yarns and thin needles for fine yarns (normally). Fat needles used with fine yarn will create loose stitches, not good for these animal patterns. Bulky yarn knitted on thin needles will create tight stitches, which would be okay for animals.

Check the Knitting Tension Chart for suggestions of what needles to use with different yarns.

KNITTING NEEDLES: *Smallest to largest*

American	000	00	0	1	2	3	4	5	6	7	8	9	10	10½	11	12	13	15
English & Canadian	15	14	13	12	11	10	9	8	7	6	5	4	3	2	2(1)	0	00	000
Metric	1.75	2	2.25	2.50	2.75/3	3.25	3.50	4	4.50	5	5.50	6	6.50	7	7.50	8	8.50	9

KNITTING TENSION (GAUGE) CHART

In making yarn animals, correct tension is not a matter of life and death. Use this chart as a general guide. Your animal will work as long as your tension is close to the figure given.

This is an average chart. Tensions are given in stockinette stitch (knit one row, purl one row). Needle sizes are given in American.

Yarn Group	Needle size	Stitches per inch	Rows per inch
Baby Yarn	1	9	(approximate!)
	2	8½	
	3	8	
Fingering Yarn	1	8	12
	2	7½	11½
	3	7	11
Sport Yarn (2-ply)	1	8½	
	2	8	
	3	7½	
Knitting Worsted	2	8–7½	10–9½
(3- to 4-ply, regular yarn)	3	7½–7	9½–9
	4	7–6½	9–8½
	5	6½–6	8½–8
	6	6–5½	8–7½
	7	5½–5	7½–7
	8	5–4½	7–6½
	9	4½–4	6½–6
	10	4–3½	5½–5
Double Knitting Yarn (close	3	6	8
to knitting worsted or use	4	5¾	7¾
doubled sport yarn)	5	5½	7½
	6	5¼	7¾
	7	5	6½
Bulky	4	5	
(doubled knitting	6	4½	
worsted or craft yarn)	8	4	
	9	3½	
Very Bulky—Rug Yarn	9	3½	
(1 strand double knitting	10	3¼	
and 1 strand bulky)	10½	3	
	13	2½	

Note: Charts showing which size needles to use with which yarn for a given size stitch and row are rarely published. There are many very good reasons. One is that it is difficult for any two people to knit with exactly the same tension. Another is that yarn manufacturers do not use the same standards. For example, one manufacturer may make a heavier knitting worsted than another. The heavier knitting worsted will work up into larger stitches and wider rows. It will also have fewer yards per ounce.

Since correct tension and a specific brand of yarn are not essential to complete any of these animals successfully, I am including the chart as a guide. Use it as an aid and not as a source of frustration!

KNITTING TENSION GAUGE FOR GARTER STITCH IN KNITTING WORSTED

Needle Size	Stitches per inch	Rows per inch
4	5	10
8	4	8
10½	3½	7

KNITTING TERMS, TECHNIQUES AND ABBREVIATIONS

In knitting there are two basic stitches—the knit stitch and the purl stitch. Everything else is a variation of those stitches. New stitch patterns are made by increasing and decreasing the number of stitches and by working with the yarn in front of or behind the work.

GARTER STITCH: If plain knitting is done back and forth for several rows, the work looks the same on both sides. The garter stitch creates rows of horizontal ridges. It is looser and stretchier than the stockinette stitch. The name "garter" stitch comes from its original use as a stretchy stitch which held up stockings. In directions, it is written: K every row.

STOCKINETTE/STOCKING STITCH: The stockinette stitch is made when you alternate knit rows with purl rows. It is the most commonly used stitch combination. The knit side is smooth and the purl side is bumpy. The knit, or smooth, side is usually the right side of the work. The name "stockinette" comes from stocking net, a stitch originally used to make stockings. In directions, it is written: K 1 row, P 1 row.

KNIT SIDE   PURL SIDE

CASTING ON: Casting on means putting the rows of loops on your needle, from which you will start to knit. There are several methods of casting on. The one shown here is also called "knitting on." Make a *slip knot*:

    Pull the piece of yarn through the loop around your fingers.

    Slide the yarn off your fingers. It will look like this.

①   ②   ③

Pull ends tightly.

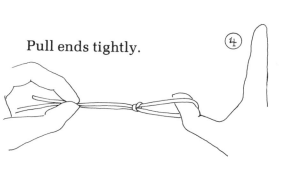

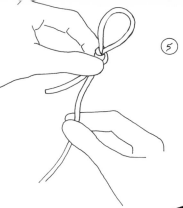

Slide the loop onto the needle you are holding in your left hand.

Now you are ready to start *casting on*. Insert the right needle from the front under the left needle and through the loop.

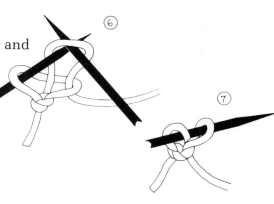

Illustration above, right shows how the needles and yarn are held. With the index finger, bring the yarn around the point of the right-hand needle.

Pull the yarn through the loop.

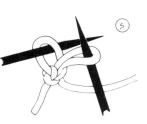

Slide the new loop from the right needle to the left needle and remove the left needle.

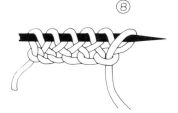

Illustration below, right shows 6 stitches cast on.

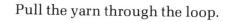

To make a neat edge, do not knit the first stitch on each row. Instead, insert the right needle behind the left needle and slip the first stitch onto the right needle.

PLAIN KNIT STITCH: To make a neat edge, do not knit the first stitch on each knit row. Instead, insert the right needle behind the left needle and slip the first stitch onto the right needle. Then begin knitting. Hold the needle with the cast-on stitches in your left hand and begin by following the same steps used in casting on.

Insert the right needle from the front, under the left needle and through the first loop on the left needle.

With the index finger, bring the yarn around the point of the right-hand needle.

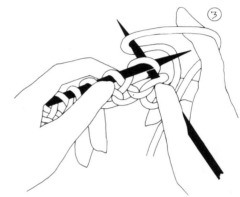

Pull the yarn through the loop and off the left needle.

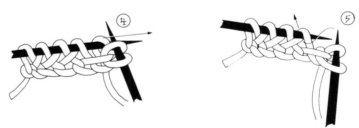

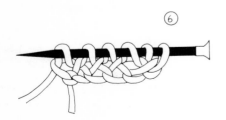

One knit stitch is complete. The arrow in illustration 5 shows how to start knitting the next stitch. Continue to the end of the row. All the stitches will now be on the right-hand needle. Illustration 6 shows the first knit row completed. It doesn't look like much but in a few more rows it will start to look like what you recognize as knitting.

166

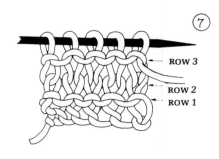

To start the *second row*, transfer the needle with the stitches to your left hand and begin again.

Illustration 7 shows what happens if you knit back and forth for several rows. It is called plain knitting or the garter stitch. Every time you complete two rows, you add another ridge to your work.

Row: When you knit from one end of the needle to the other you have made a row.

RIDGE: Two knit rows together make a ridge.

PURL STITCH: The purl stitch is hardly ever used alone. It is combined with the knit stitch to create the stockinette stitch. Just as in plain knitting you start by holding the needle with the stitches in your left hand. The differences between knitting and purling are that (1) in purling the yarn is in front of the work instead of coming from behind and (2) the right needle is inserted into the loop from the right side instead of from the left. Also, you don't slip the first stitch in the row.

Insert the right needle into the loop from the right side.

Wrap the yarn around the right needle from the front.

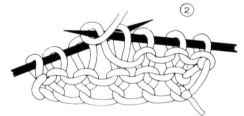

Draw the loop through the stitch.

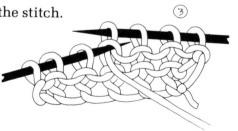

Slide the new loop off the left needle and insert the right needle into the right side of the next loop to start purling the next stitch.

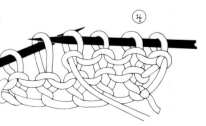

167

KNIT VS. K (k): "Knit" means to do the stockinette stitch unless otherwise specified. "K" and "k" mean to knit a row rather than "P" or "p" (purl) a row.

INCREASE (Inc.): Knit (or purl) into the front of a stitch but leave the stitch on the left needle. Then knit (or purl) into the back of the same stitch and slip the stitch off the left-hand needle. You have increased by one stitch.

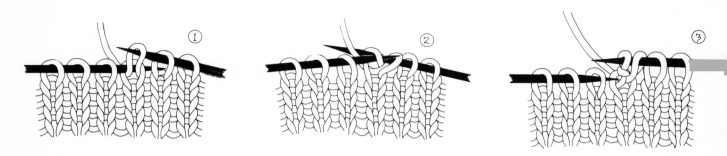

DECREASE (Dec): Knit (or purl) two stitches together as if they were one stitch.

WORK EVEN: Work without increases or decreases, using the stitch which has been described.

(. . .): Parentheses mean to repeat the instructions between them as many times as specified. For example "(k 2, p 2) 4 times" would mean to follow the instructions between the parentheses a total of 4 times.

JOINING YARNS: Join a new ball of yarn at the beginning of a row. You can tie the new end to the old end and weave the ends into the work later. If you are running out of yarn and the only way you'll have enough is to join the new yarn in the middle of a row, don't panic. A knot in the middle of a row may show slightly but it won't affect the appearance of the animal. Remember to pull the knot through to the back of the work.

CHANGING COLORS: Unless the pattern calls for color changes within a row (as for the porcupine's pattern), always change colors at the beginning of a knit row. Never change colors at the beginning of a purl row. If you are changing colors in a garter stitch pattern (as for the elephant), always change colors on the same side, the side which will later be the "right" side. Mark the right side with a safety pin so you'll know which is which.

DROPPED STITCHES: Sometimes you make the unfortunate discovery that you have dropped a stitch. You'll see a little "ladder" running down your work to the dropped stitch. If the knit side is facing you, stick a crochet hook through the dropped stitch and pull the yarn from the row above through the loop. You will have a new loop. Keep repeating that until you are up to the row you are working on. Slide the new loop onto the needle and continue on your way. Picking up purl stitches works almost the same way. See illustration 2.

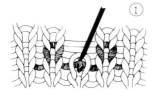 

RIPPING OUT YOUR WORK: On these projects sometimes you can convince yourself that a mistake isn't serious enough to warrant ripping back and starting again. Sometimes you can't. So resign yourself and rip. You'll find that ripping is a lot easier than knitting. Slow down when you reach the last row you have to rip and pull out those stitches one at a time, picking up each stitch on a needle. It is easier to pick up stitches on a needle which is thinner than the one you are using, but the one you are using will work perfectly well. Stick the needle through the picked-up loops from the front. If you don't get the loops on the needle correctly, they won't be in the right position to knit and you'll have to turn them around when you come to them.

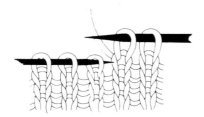

BINDING OFF/CASTING OFF: Binding off is the term used for ending your work.

Knit two stitches. Slide the point of the left-hand needle into the far stitch on the right-hand needle. Lift the first stitch over the second stitch as the arrow indicates in illustration 1. The two stitches are now combined into one stitch on the right-hand needle.

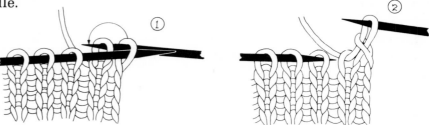

Knit a second stitch onto the right needle. Lift the first stitch over the second. Continue the same procedure across the row.

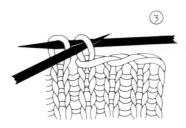

When you have reached the last stitch, cut the yarn about 4″ from the work and pull it through the loop.

BLOCKING: Although blocking isn't necessary for knitted animals, it does make them look extra good. Block each piece separately, before sewing together. Lay pieces wrong side up on ironing board. Pin them down. Iron with a moderately hot iron over a damp cloth. Do not press down. Let the pieces dry completely before joining them.

Note: Never iron Orlon yarns.

SEWING TOGETHER: Edges can be sewn together in several ways. In knitting they are normally whipstitched together. They can be woven together or back stitched together. For an interesting effect you might try feather stitching or buttonhole stitching them together from the outside. If you are stitching the pieces together, use a large, blunt-pointed needle with a large eye. They are called yarn needles and tapestry needles. Edges can also be slip stitched together or single crocheted together. Single crocheting done on the right side gives a nice, ridged effect.

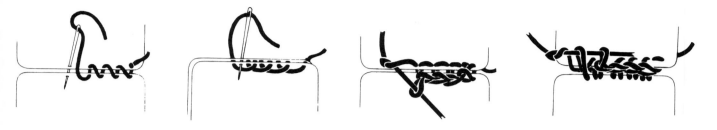

CORRECT YARN TENSION: If the stitch is just loose enough to allow the needles to slip through the work easily, your yarn tension is neither too tight nor too loose.

KNITTING TO A SPECIFIC GAUGE/TENSION: Knit a sample about 3″ square, using the yarn and needles specified in the instructions. With a ruler, measure an inch horizontally and count the number of stitches. Measure an inch vertically and count the number of rows. If you have too many stitches and rows per inch, try using larger needles. If there are too few stitches, use smaller needles. Experiment with different needles until you have the correct number of stitches and rows per square inch.

Some people knit to one tension and purl to another tension. If that's your problem, use needles in two different sizes.

WHERE CAN YOU FIND OUT ABOUT CORRECT GAUGE? Check the wrapper on your yarn. Often an average gauge is included in the information. Patterns for clothing always have the gauge indicated. These animals don't because it isn't that important. As long as you work to an even tension the animal will turn out fine; exact size doesn't matter.

There are Knitting Tension Charts on pp. 163 and 164 to help if you are concerned.

KNITTING TERMS	ABBREVIATIONS
Knit (as compared to purl)	K, k
Purl	P, p
Stitch(es)	st
Slip	sl
Slip Stitch	sl st
Increase	inc
Decrease	dec
Beginning	beg

KNITTING TERMS	ABBREVIATIONS
Yarn Over	yo
Together	tog
Round	rnd
Ounces	oz
Stockinette Stitch	st st
Main Color	MC
Contrasting Color	CC
Loop	lp

HOW TO DESIGN YOUR OWN KNIT PATTERN

Design an animal pattern in muslin or use any animal pattern from a book or magazine. Draw the outlines of all the pattern pieces on tracing paper.

Lay the tracing paper sketch over the graph you want to use, paper clipping it in place. Then count the squares representing stitches that fall inside the outline, row by row. Write down the instructions or work directly from the sketch.

For example, if there are 16 squares in the first row, 18 squares in the 2nd and 3rd rows and 13 squares in the 4th row, you would write it like this:

Cast on 16 st.

Row 1: K 16.

Row 2: Inc 2 at beg and end of row (or wherever the stitches should be added). (18 st.)

Row 3: K even.

Row 4: Dec 5 (evenly spaced) or (at beg of row) (depending on where the stitches should be eliminated). (13 st.)

Graph sections at left are actual size. Both graphs are for average tension, using #8 knitting needles and knitting worsted. If you want to use the stockinette graph, knit up a test square, changing needle sizes if necessary, until you end up with 5 stitches per inch and 7 rows per inch. Garter stitch graph tension is 4 stitches per inch and 8 rows per inch. Trace and extend these sections to size desired.

Illustration on p. 173 shows how to use the graph.

You're probably going to need a larger sheet of graph paper than you want to draw. Make several Xerox copies of your graph and tape them together. Or divide the pattern into large rectangles the size of the entire sheet of graph paper and work the pattern out section by section.

STOCKINETTE STITCH

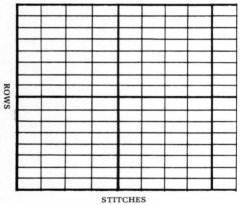

ROWS

STITCHES

GARTER STITCH

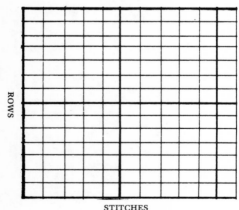

ROWS

STITCHES

HOW TO MAKE YOUR OWN GRAPH FOR ANY STITCH, YARN OR NEEDLES

If you work to a different tension or if you want to use different yarn or needles, design your own graph. Knit a sample square about 3″ on each side. Measure 1″ horizontally and count the stitches. Measure 1″ vertically and count the rows.

Divide each inch across one side of the paper into as many parts as there are stitches to the inch. Draw vertical lines from those points. Mark that edge "Stitches."

Turn the paper the other way and divide each inch across that side into as many parts as there are rows to the inch. Draw vertical lines from those points. Mark that edge "Rows."

Turn the paper so the "Stitches" side is facing you. Use the graph in the manner described above.

GRAPH FOR GARTER STITCH

Do a test square to check your garter stitch tension. If it works out to twice as many rows as stitches per inch it is easy to make over a regular sheet of graph paper into a garter stitch graph. Just draw horizontal lines between the lines in one direction. Mark the side with the extra divisions "Rows" and mark the side without the divisions "Stitches." If your tension is not a 2 to 1 ratio, follow the "How to Make Your Own Graph" instructions.

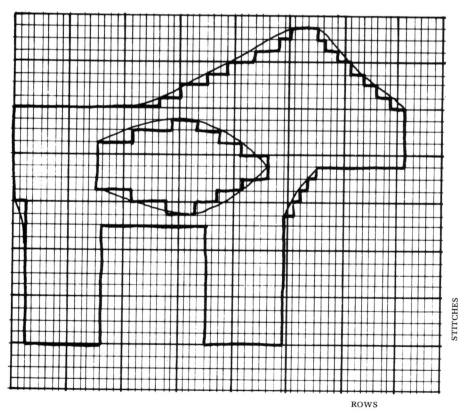

STITCHES

ROWS

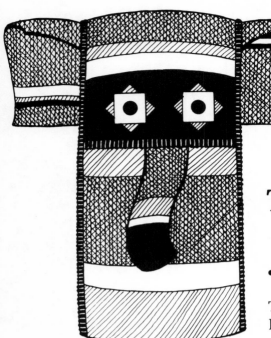

The Projects

• KNIT ELEPHANT

The elephant is an excellent project for someone who wants to learn how to knit. It is as easy to make as a scarf and at least twice as much fun. The entire project is done in plain knitting, only the garter stitch! You don't have to learn how to purl or increase or decrease. And the variations are all just as easy to make.

MATERIALS

> #8 knitting needles
> 3 oz. knitting worsted. Use one color or as many colors as you like. The elephant looks good in stripes. Always change colors on the same side. (Mark that side with a safety pin.) If you don't, there will be a row of dots in the new color running through the old color before the stripe starts.
> Felt scraps for eyes
> Yarn needle
> White glue
> Stuffing

■	BLACK
▨	PURPLE
◫	ORANGE
▢	YELLOW

BODY: Cast on 30 stitches. Knit 180 rows. Cast off.

EARS: Make 2. Cast on 15 stitches. Knit 36 rows. Cast off.

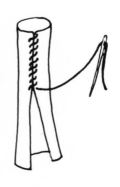

TRUNK: Cast on 12 stitches. Knit 40 rows. Cast off. Whipstitch the long sides of the trunk together to make a tube.

    To assemble, whipstitch the narrow ends of the body strip together. Stitch the trunk on at the middle of the seam. Whipstitch the sides of the body shut, stuffing the body before it is sewn shut. Fold over the inside top corners of the ears and whipstitch them

174

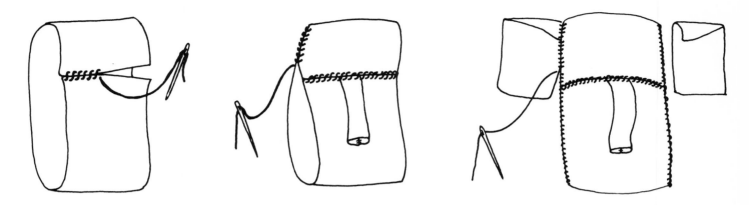

onto the body. Cut eyes out of felt and glue or sew them on. Use the eye pattern shown here or design your own. Finish by tieing a little braided tail to the back side of the elephant.

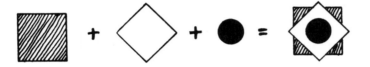

Variations

The knit owl, cat and turtle are based on the elephant. Try designing other animals based on squares, rectangles and tubes.

P.S. The elephant won 1st prize in the Junior Division for knitting at the Burks Falls Fair. The owl won 2nd prize in the Stuffed Animal Division.

• KNIT OWL

This is a simple variation of the elephant. Use the garter stitch. There are two ways to make legs for the owl if you want them. They can be cut out of felt or crocheted using the chain stitch. The chain stitch is the beginning crochet stitch and is very easy to do.

MATERIALS
    3 oz. knitting worsted in body color
    1 oz. knitting worsted in face color
    2 oz. knitting worsted in wing color

Small amount of yellow or orange yarn for beak (and legs, if crocheted)
#8 knitting needles
Scraps of black and white yarn or felt for eyes
Stuffing
Yarn needle
#H crochet hook (if you want crocheted legs) or felt for legs

BODY: Cast on 60 stitches. Knit 180 rows. Cast off.

FACE: Cast on 30 stitches. Knit 60 rows. Cast off.

WINGS: Make 2. Cast on 25 stitches. Knit 63 rows. Cast off.

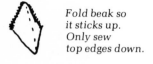

Fold beak so it sticks up. Only sew top edges down.

BEAK: Cast on 12 stitches. Knit 20 rows. Cast off.

LEGS: Not necessary but fun. Crochet 2. Double the yellow yarn and ch 12. End off. With the yarn still doubled, ch 4. Slip stitch into 5th ch on the first chained piece and ch 4 again. End off. (Cut legs out of felt if you prefer.)

To assemble, fold body piece so it is 30 stitches wide. Sew body like a pillow, stuffing it. Sew the face near the upper part of the body, putting a little stuffing behind it. Sew the beak to the face, folding it slightly in the middle so it sticks out. Sew the narrow ends of the wings to the sides of the body. Tie on the feet (if used) so they dangle down. Add eyes and that's it.

• CAT
(Variation of elephant)

MATERIALS
  #8 knitting needles
  3 oz. knitting worsted
  Stuffing
  Yarn and felt bits

BODY: Cast on 30 stitches. Knit 28″ in garter stitch (plain knitting). Cast off. Stuff and sew like a pillow.

EARS: Make 2. Cast on 10 stitches. Knit 20 rows, or until you have a square. Cast off.

Fold ears, corner to corner. Stuff and sew up the sides. Sew ears to top of body.

To assemble, check the illustration.

Add a face and whiskers.

Braid a tail and tie to the back of the cat.

Run a heavy piece of yarn or ribbon around the neck to gather it in. Tie in a bow.

EARS

• TURTLE
(Variation of elephant)

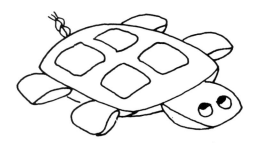

MATERIALS
    #8 knitting needles
    2 oz. knitting worsted for body
    2 oz. knitting worsted for legs, head and patches on shell in a
    different color.
    Stuffing
    Yarn or felt bits for face

BODY: Cast on 28 stitches. Knit 16". Cast off. Stuff and sew like a pillow.

HEAD: Cast on 30 stitches in second color. Knit 4". Cast off. Stuff and sew like a little pillow. Sew to front of body.

LEGS: Make 4. Cast on 15 stitches in second color. Knit 4". Cast off. Stuff and sew like a little pillow. Sew to sides of body.

BACK PATCHES: Knit 4 little squares or crochet 4 little granny squares in colors which would look good on the body or in second color. Sew them to the turtle's back.

TAIL: Braid a little tail in the second color and tie to back of turtle.

FACE: Make a face like the one in illustration above.

• ANY-ANIMAL PUPPET

This is a beginner's project. It adds the purl stitch to the knit stitch but there's still no increasing or decreasing necessary. The nice thing about our puppet is that you can make it into any animal you want. Check the list of variations before you start.

MATERIALS
#8 knitting needles
#G crochet hook
Any scraps of knitting worsted

BASIC BODY: Cast on 30 st (6″). Knit 63 rows (9″) in stockinette stitch. Cast off.

Sew the 9″ edges together to make a tube.

Flatten the tube so the sewn seam is at one edge. Then sew 1½″ of the opening opposite the seam together.

Finally, sew the rest of the opening shut so the side seam and the top seam meet in the middle.

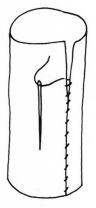
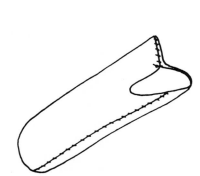
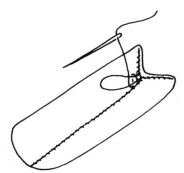

EARS: Make 2. Use a contrasting color so they show up. Cut them out of felt or knit as follows. Cast on 8 st. Knit 18 rows. Dec 1 at Row 7, 8, 11, 12, 15 and 16. End off at Row 18. Sew on ears as shown in illustration at top of page.

EYES: Make 2 (or 1 for a Cyclops). Cut them out of felt or crochet them. Using white or contrasting color yarn, ch 2. Make 6 sc in 2nd ch from hook.

Rnd 2: 2 sc in each sc around. (12 sc.) End off. Attach eyes to puppet with a French knot or satin stitch in black yarn or other contrasting color.

HAIR (optional): Wrap yarn around 3 fingers 8 times. Tie yarn tightly in middle. Clip loops and tie hair to top of head. Brush or unravel yarn strands to make hair fluffy.

NOSE: Embroider a nose or tie on a mini-pompom.

Variations

Variations are endless. Crochet a ridge down the puppet's back to make a dragon. Crochet teeth. Turn it into a lion by tieing loops of yarn all around the head to make a mane. Knit the body in black and orange stripes and make green eyes for a tiger. Add whiskers or a moustache to the end of the nose. Make the body longer to cover more of your arm. Make big, floppy dog ears. Add a tongue. Make felt or button eyes. In no time you will have a menagerie of puppets.

• MR. BIG-MOUTH PUPPET

Here's our easy version of the puppet who gobbles all the other puppets up. Get out your bag of left-over yarn and see what you end up with.

MATERIALS

Use whatever yarn and needles you want. To work the puppet up extra fast, use big needles and bulky yarn or knit several strands of knitting worsted together.

Knit a strip 3½" wide and 22" long, the first 8" in body color, the next 6" in red or other mouth color and the last 8" in body color.
Stitch up the puppet as shown in illustration below.
Decorate by using suggestions listed under Variations for the Any-Animal Puppet.

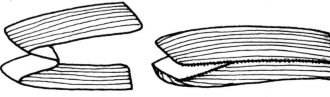

Stitch up the puppet as shown.

• FINGER PUPPETS

Karen insisted that finger puppets had to be included. They are fast and very much loved by small children. Make them out of any left-over ends of yarn and decorate them with bits of yarn, felt, ribbon, lace, buttons, beads, sequins, etc., etc., etc. The directions are for knitting worsted and #8 needles. Anything close may be substituted.

180

ELEPHANT

Body: Cast on 15. Knit 12 rows. Cast off. Sew together purl side out.

Ears: Cast on 6. Knit 4 rows. Cast off.

Trunk: Chain 6. Sl st back up chain. Or cast on 6, knit 1 row and cast off.

Sew pieces together and make a face.

MOUSE

Body: Cast on 12. Knit 11 rows. Cast off. Sew together to fit over your finger.

Ears: Knit or crochet tiny ears. Or cut them out of felt.

Sew pieces together and make a face. Braid a tail and arms.

GIRAFFE

Body: Cast on 10. Knit 12 rows even. Inc 3 st at beg each of next 2 rows. Knit 3 rows even. Cast off. Sew up seams.

Mane: Rya stitch or knot yarn along the neck.

LION

Body: Cast on 10. Knit 9 rows even. Inc 2 at beg next 2 rows. Knit 5 rows even. Cast off.

Mane: Rya stitch or knot yarn around back of head and under chin.

OCTOPUS

The octopus is crocheted but you could knit up a head by casting on 10 and knitting 8 rows even and sewing across top and down one side.

Body: Ch 6. Sl st tog. Ch 1. Sc around.

Rnd 2: 2 sc in each sc around.

Rnds 3–4: Work even.

Rnds 5–6: Dec every sc. End off.

Legs: Make 8 tight braids around the bottom of the body. Use 3 strands of yarn doubled for each braid.

DOG

Body: Cast on 10. Knit 11 rows even. Inc 4 st at beg of each of next 2 rows. Knit 4 rows even. Cast off. Sew up seams.

Ears: Knit 2 big ears in a contrasting color. Cast on 8. Knit 4 rows. Cast off. Or make ears out of felt.

Variations

You can see how easy it is to make finger puppets from these patterns. If you want to try something really different, knit a glove with each finger a different color and kind of animal.

181

• DONKEY

This is another easy-to-make garter-stitch animal with some simple crocheting also required. Check all the variations. Once you realize how easy it is to make one, you'll probably want to make several others.

MATERIALS

    2 oz. gray knitting worsted
    1 oz. white knitting worsted
    Bits of black yarn
    #8 knitting needles
    #G crochet hook
    Stuffing
    Bits of felt for face

BODY: Work from nose to tail. Use gray yarn. Make 2. Cast on 5 st. K 2 rows. Inc 1 at end of Row 2. Continue straight knitting, increasing 1 at end of each even-numbered row through Row 12. (11 st.)

Rows 13–18: Inc 1 at end of Rows 13, 15, 16 and 17. (15 st.)

Row 19: Inc 13 at end of row to start leg. (28 st.)

Rows 20–33: Dec 1 at end of Rows 20, 24, 28 and 32 for neck slope. (24 st.)

Row 34: Dec 10 at beg of row to end front leg.

Row 35–36: K even.

Row 37–45: Dec 1 at end of Rows 37, 41 and 45.

Row 46–48: K even.

Row 49: Inc 10 at end of row to start hind leg. (21 st.)

Rows 50–61: K even.

Row 62: Cast off 12 at beg of row to end leg. K 1 row. Cast off and end off.

STOMACH: Make 2. Work in white. Work from front to back. Cast on 2. K 2 rows. Cast on 12 for leg. K 11 rows even.

> *Row 14:* Cast off 10 to end front leg. K 16 rows even.
> *Row 30:* Cast on 10 for hind leg. K 12 rows even. Cast off.

FACE: Work in white. Cast on 2 st. K 34 rows. Inc 1 at Rows 5, 6, 11 and 12. Dec 1 at Rows 22, 23, 28 and 29. Cast off at Row 34 and end off.

> Sew donkey together and stuff.

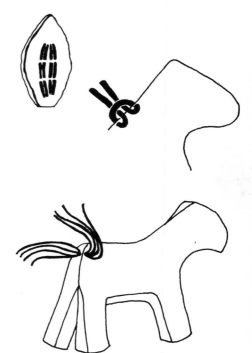

NOSE: Crochet in black. Ch 3. Sl st tog. Ch 1. (2 sc in 1st ch. Sc in next ch) around.

> *Rnds 2–4:* (2 sc in 1st sc. Sc in next sc) around. End off. Stuff and sew to face.

EARS: Gray with black inside. Cast on 4 st. K 20 rows. Inc 1 at Rows 3, 4, 7 and 8. Dec 1 at Rows 11, 12, 15, 16, 19 and 20. End off.

> Thread black yarn on a needle and weave it up and down the inside of each ear. Sew on ears. See illustration p. 182.

MANE: Black. Use a crochet hook to loop short lengths of yarn from the center of the forehead down the back of the neck. Make 2 or 3 rows. Clip the mane so it is about ½″ long. Or make rya stitch loops for the mane. The rya stitch is faster than hooking.

TAIL: Black. Pull six 8″ lengths of black yarn halfway through the same stitch where you want the tail to be. Braid the lengths and tie around the ends.

HOOVES: Black. Make 4. Ch 4. Sl st tog. 2 sc in each ch around.

> *Rnd 2:* 2 sc in each sc around. (16 sc.)
> *Rnds 3–4:* Work even. End off.
> Crochet the rounds to the bottom of each leg.

Variations

PONY

Make the pony's body, stomach, face and ears in one color. Make a long, white mane by hooking 6″ lengths of yarn to the head and along the back of the neck. Or make mane using rya stitch. Make a white tassel tail out of twelve 6″ lengths of yarn, tied at the middle and then tied to the pony. Make a white nose. Make hooves black or white.

EARS: Cast on 5. K 13 rows. Dec 1 at end of Rows 6, 9, 10 and 13. Tie off and sew to head.

UNICORN

Make the unicorn just like the pony except everything should be white. Make a white braided tail and add a horn to the top of the unicorn's head.

HORN: Cast on 4. K 19 rows. Dec 1 at Rows 9 and 10. Sew up the side and sew to forehead.

For a different effect, make the mane, tail and hooves in gold or in another color of your choice.

ZEBRA

Because it is striped, the zebra has a right and wrong side. That makes it necessary to reverse the body pieces as you would on the fronts of a cardigan. Alternate between black and white yarn every 4th row on the body pieces, starting with black. Change to white on 5th row on second side and every 4th row from then on. Make black donkey ears with white inside. Make face and stomach pieces white. Finish with a black and white braided tail and a short black donkey mane. Make the hooves black.

• PORCUPINE

He's especially cute with the easy pattern two-color stomach.
Check Method 1 for making porcupine quills. Even if you've never
tried the rya stitch before, it's faster than using a crochet hook.
Don't forget to check the variation suggestions for this pattern. You
might want to make a collection of these little animals for someone.

MATERIALS

    #8 needles
    Knitting worsted, 2 oz. one color or 1 oz. each of two colors
    Stuffing
    Yarn and felt bits for face
    #G crochet hook and small piece of cardboard, 2″ wide
    or Rya needle

ONE-COLOR PORCUPINE

BODY: Make 2. Cast on 18 st. Knit 17 rows.
    Rows 18–28: Cast off 1 st each row.
Then cast off 2 st each row to last 3 st. Bind off.

TAIL: Cast on 18 st. Knit 6 rows. Cast off.

BOTTOM: Crochet a circle 3″ in diameter. Follow Knit Rabbit's foot
instructions if you need help making the circle.

PRICKLY PORCUPINE QUILLS, METHOD 1: Make rya stitch loops
about 1½″ long all the way across the back section, rounding the
loops off to a peak at the 8th row from the top. Stitch loops through
one side of the tail strip until it looks nice and fluffy. This is the
fastest and easiest method.

PRICKLY PORCUPINE QUILLS, METHOD 2: Wrap yarn around a piece of cardboard 2″ wide. Clip yarn along one side. With a crochet hook, loop pieces of yarn all the way across the back section, rounding the loops off to a peak at the 8th row from the top. Then hook loops through one side of the tail strip until it looks nice and fluffy.

PUTTING THE PORCUPINE TOGETHER: Sew body pieces and bottom together, stuffing before you sew it shut. Sew on the tail, fluffy side up. Embroider eyes, nose and whiskers.

TWO-COLOR PORCUPINE (with checkered belly)

CHECKER STITCH

Row 1: K 2 in color #1. K 2 in color #2. Continue alternating colors every 2 st across row.
Row 2: P 2 in color #2, P 2 in color #1, cont. alternating.
Row 3: K 2 in color #2, K 2 in color #1, cont. alternating.
Row 4: P 2 in color #1, P 2 in color #2, cont. alternating.

FRONT OF BODY: Cast on 18 st. K following the directions for the one-color porcupine but use two-color checker stitch instead.

BACK OF BODY: Cast on 18 st. K in one color to Row 22. Then do the last 8 rows in checker stitch.

LOOPS: Cut strips of yarn in both colors and mix them up, hooking porcupine following directions for one-color porcupine. Or thread a rya needle with both colors and rya-stitch loops.

Note: If you want to be able to bend the nose down more, hook a pipe cleaner over the place where the nose would be and bend to the shape you want. Cover the place where the pipe cleaner shows with a satin stitch nose (see mouse illustration).

VARIATIONS
You might want to borrow arm, foot, ear and, for all but the mouse, tail patterns from the woolly squeezable squirrel for these variations.

SKUNK
Use the checker pattern to make the skunk. Rya-stitch or hook black loops along the outside of the back and tail and make a wide white stripe down the middle.

HEDGEHOG
Knit the hedgehog in brown, plain or checkered. Rya-stitch or hook

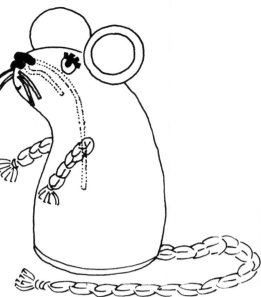

the back and tail in a mixture of any of the following colors: light brown, dark brown, black, white, beige, rust.

CHIPMUNK

Knit the chipmunk in reddish-brown with two beige vertical stripes down his back and a beige oval on the front for his stomach. Rya-stitch or hook loops only on the tail, continuing the stripes with the loops.

MOUSE

Knit up a little gray or white mouse. Crochet round ears. Braid a long tail and make 2 thick little braids for paws.

• RABBIT

This pattern is based on a rabbit I have cherished for nearly thirty years. The sawdust is coming out of his head so he's very glad to have a long-legged knit friend to take over the responsibility of rough-housing with my little boy.

All you need to know is how to increase and decrease in knitting and how to single crochet.

MATERIALS
   #8 knitting needles
   #G crochet hook
   4 oz. knitting worsted in color #1 (beige)
   4 oz. knitting worsted in color #2 (white)
   Stuffing
   Yarn needle
   Bits of yarn for face

Note: Work in stockinette stitch unless otherwise indicated.

FACE: Cast on 16 st in color #2. Inc 1 st in middle of each K row to 24 st. Dec 1 st in middle of each K row to 20 st. Cast off 1 st at beg of every row (K and P) to 9 st. Cast off.

BACK OF HEAD (Made like a baby bonnet—see illustration above). Cast on 50 st in color #2. Knit 12 rows. K 2 tog every 5th st and K first 2 and last 2 tog on each K row for 6 K rows. (Work as close as possible to these instructions. Some of the rows won't come out exactly even but that's okay.) K 2 tog every other st to 7 st. Cast off by running a piece of yarn through last 7 st and tying tog in a tight circle.

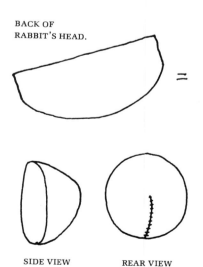

BACK OF
RABBIT'S HEAD.

SIDE VIEW   REAR VIEW

EARS: Make 4, 2 in color #1 and 2 in color #2. Cast on 6 st. Inc 1 st in the middle of each K row to 17 st. Dec 1 st in the middle of each K row to 8 st. K 2 tog all the way across for 2 K rows. Cast off.

Crochet ear pieces tog, leaving bottom open. You might want to sew a piece of stiffening fabric inside ears to help them stand straighter.

CHEST: Cast on 32 st in color #1. Knit 6½". Cast off 1" on either side and knit 1" farther, casting off 1 st on each row. Cast off.

BACK: The bottom of the back is like the heel of a sock. Cast on 36 st in color #1. Start to dec every row beginning at 2nd K row—dec to 22 st. Pick up 7 st on each side to 36 st again (like a sock). K 4". Cast off 1" on either side and knit 1" farther, casting off 1 st on each row. Cast off.

ARMS: Make 2. Cast on 20 st in color #1. Knit 5½". Change to color #2 and knit 2½" more. Cast off.

Sew the hand and side of arm together, leaving the top of the arm open.

LEGS: Make 2. Cast on 23 st in color #1. Knit 10½". Change to color #2 and knit 3" more, increasing 2 on each K row. Cast off. Sew up long side of leg.

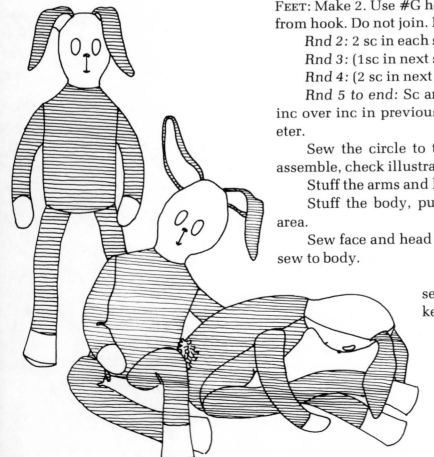

FEET: Make 2. Use #G hook and color #2. Ch 2. Work 6 sc in 2nd ch from hook. Do not join. Mark beg of rows.

Rnd 2: 2 sc in each sc. (12 sc.)

Rnd 3: (1sc in next sc. 2 sc in next sc) 6 times. (18 sc.)

Rnd 4: (2 sc in next sc. 1 sc in each of next 2 sc) 6 times. (24 sc.)

Rnd 5 to end: Sc around. Inc 6 every rnd, being careful not to inc over inc in previous rnd. Continue until circle is 3¼" in diameter.

Sew the circle to the bottom of the leg to complete foot. To assemble, check illustration at left.

Stuff the arms and legs and sew to body.

Stuff the body, putting a little extra stuffing in the stomach area.

Sew face and head together, leaving neck open. Stuff head and sew to body.

Tuck 1" of bottom of ear inside itself and sew ears to head. The tucked-in part helps keep the ears standing up.

RABBIT FACE: Embroider features on rabbit's face. Start the nose where the decreasing stitches begin. See illustration for ideas.

TAIL: Wind color #2 yarn around a 2½″ wide piece of cardboard 100 times. Clip both sides and tie together tightly in the middle. Tie tail to back of rabbit.

• MOTHER KANGAROO AND BABY

(Shown on p. 190)

Although this looks like a difficult pattern it is actually quite easy. I can say that now, because five people struggled with it until it really did work. All you need to know is the garter stitch (plain knitting) and how to increase and decrease. Increasing in this pattern is limited to casting on and decrease (in case you haven't tried it before) means to knit two stitches together instead of knitting them one at a time (see p. 168).

MATERIALS

#5 to #8 knitting needles (#5 makes a smaller, tighter-stitched animal)
4 oz. knitting worsted in body color
2 oz. knitting worsted in lighter color than body
Stuffing
Bits of yarn and/or felt for faces.

Mother Kangaroo

Note: Work in garter stitch (plain knitting).

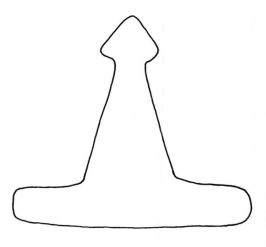

BODY: Cast on 84 st in body color. K 15 rows. Slip 1st st on each row. Illustration right shows what body piece will look like. Cast off 22 st at beg of next 2 rows (40 st left in middle). K straight for 38 rows. (K 19, K 2 tog, K rest of row. K next row plain) 2 times. (K 18, K 2 tog, K rest of row. K next row plain) 2 times. Continue to dec pattern this way until you K 8, K 2 tog for 2nd time. (16 st.) K 4 rows straight. Cast on 7 st end of next 2 rows. (30 st.) K 2 rows. K 2 tog at beg next 18 rows. (12 st.) Run thread through st. Pull tog and tie off.

BOTTOM: Use light color yarn. Cast on 15 st. K 16 rows. K 7. K 2 tog. K rest of row. (K 6. K 2 tog. K rest of row) 2 times. (K 5. K 2 tog. K rest of row) 2 times. Continue to dec in this manner until all st are decreased. End off.

FRONT: Use light color yarn. Cast on 60 st. K 12 rows. Cast off 21 st at beg of next 2 rows. (18 st left in middle.) K 33 rows. Cast off.

On same row as legs were cast off, pick up 18 st in the middle of the row. K 34 rows. (K 8 st. K 2 tog. K rest of row. K next row plain) 2 times. (K 7 st. K 2 tog. K rest of row. K next row plain) 2 times. Continue to dec this way until 3 st left. K 3 tog. End off.

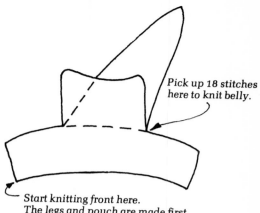

Pick up 18 stitches here to knit belly.

Start knitting front here. The legs and pouch are made first.

TAIL: Use body color. Cast on 24 st. K 20 rows. (K 11. K 2 tog. K rest of row. K next row plain) 2 times. (K 10. K 2 tog. K rest of row. K next row plain) 2 times. Repeat decreases until all st used up. Sew up, stuff and attach.

ARMS: Make 2. Use body color. Cast on 16, K 3″ or about 20 rows. Cast off.

Sew up side and end of arm. Stuff and attach.

EARS: Make 2. Use body color. Cast on 12 st. K 2 rows. K 2 tog at beg of every row until all st are decreased.

To assemble, sew the head at the top of the back. Sew pouch to front. Sew front to back. Stuff, adding a little extra stuffing to the neck area and at the bottom. Sew on bottom, arms, tail and ears. Embroider eyes and nose in contrasting colors or make from felt and glue on. Knot a few pieces of yarn to the top of her head for hair.

Baby Kangaroo: Use same materials as for mother.

BODY: Cast on 25 st. K 8 rows. Cast off 7 st at beg of next 2 rows. (11 st.) K 16 rows. Cast on 4 st at beg of next 2 rows. K 3 rows. K 2 tog at beg and end of every row for 5 rows. Run a thread through the remaining 7 st and tie off.

FRONT: Cast on 20 st. K 8 rows. Cast off 7 st at beg next 2 rows. (6 st.) K 2 rows. K 2 tog at beg every row until all st are off. End off.

TAIL: Cast on 8 st. K 8 rows. (K 3. K 2 tog. K rest of row. K next row plain) 2 times. Continue to dec this way until all st are off. Sew up middle and stuff.

ARMS: Make 2. Cast on 6 st. K 14 rows. Cast off. Sew and stuff.

EARS: Make 2. Cast on 5 st. K 4 rows. K 2 tog at beg each row until all st are off.

To assemble, sew together from head down, adding front panel. Stuff. Sew on stuffed arms and tail. Embroider eyes and nose or make out of felt. Add a tuft of yarn to top of head for hair. Tuck him in his mother's pouch.

VARIATIONS

How about designing an extra large pouch for the mother kangaroo and putting in twins? You might run a drawstring across top of pouch.

DRAGON: (Variation of mother kangaroo—the materials are the same). Use #8 knitting needles. Use green yarn for the back, arms, ears and tail. Use yellow yarn for the front and bottom. Use red yarn for the ridge down the dragon's back.

All the parts of the dragon are knit the same as the kangaroo except for the front. If you want to make a Mother Dragon with a pouch, make the front the same as the kangaroo.

Front: Cast on 60 st. K 12 rows. Cast off 21 st at beg of next 2 rows. (18 st left in middle.) K 34 rows even. (K 8 st. K 2 tog. K rest of row. K next row even) 2 times. (K 7 st. K 2 tog. K rest of row. K next row even) 2 times. Continue to dec this way until 3 st are left. K 3 tog.

Ridge: Use red knitting worsted and #8 needles. Make the ridge long enough to go from the forehead, down the dragon's back and to the end of the tail. Cast on 2 st. K 1 row even. (Inc 1 st at beg of row. K rest of row. K next row even) 2 times. Inc in this manner until 6 st on needle. K 1 row even. (K 2 tog. K rest of row. K next row even) 2 times. Dec in this manner until 2 st remain. K 1 row even and start the next peak in the ridge. Make 10 peaks. For the last 2, continue the same only with 5 st on the second to the last and 4 st on the last peak. End off and sew to dragon.

Mouth: Cast on 10 st in green. K 4½". Cast off. Fold in half and sew, unstuffed, horizontally across front of face. Make a black or red french knot on each top corner of nose. (See illustration.)

Tongue: Cast on 10 st in red. K 1 row and cast off. Sew to mouth.

BABY DRAGON: If you want to make a baby dragon, make him in the same colors as the mother. Slip stitch a red ridge down the baby's back and then go back up the ridge alternating in single and double crochet.

DINOSAUR (Variation on dragon). Make exactly the same as the dragon except leave off the mouth and make the ridge green.

VII
CROCHETED ANIMALS

"Crochet" is the French word for "hook." Crochet and knitting are both ways of working with loops. In crochet, one loop is pulled through another and then another with a hook to make chains which grow into potholders, scarves, sweaters, animals, etc. Crochet is a freer, more creative way of working with loops than knitting. Instead of being limited to rows or tubes, you can hook off in any direction by adding chains in any number, starting and stopping and turning back on your work wherever you wish. You can crochet any shape you can dream up, either flat or enclosing an area. In deciding what materials to use, remember that you can crochet anything that bends easily. According to archaeologists, early man crocheted baskets out of bark fibers. And don't let the patterns here limit you. I started to crochet a fish one afternoon and it had turned into a hat for my baby by evening. The same thing could happen to you if you suddenly decided to try the walrus' body on your head before it's half finished. Fold the sides up and see how you like it. Anything can happen with a crochet hook.

• ATTENTION CROCHETERS

Before you start any of the following patterns, do you know whether you crochet *American*, *Canadian* or *English*? American and Canadian are the same. English is different. The English stitch name is always one stitch larger than the American and Canadian. See "Crochet Terms" chart to compare American/Canadian stitches with English stitches. Directions in this book are for American crochet.

Note to Canadians: Being Canadian doesn't mean that you automatically crochet Canadian. You might crochet English.

General Directions

CROCHET TERMS AND ABBREVIATIONS

American & Canadian	Abbreviation	English	Abbreviation
Slip stitch	sl st	Single crochet	sc
Single crochet	sc	Double crochet	dc
Half double	hdc or h dc	Half treble	htr
Double crochet	dc	Treble	tr
Treble	tr	Double treble	dbl. tr.
Double treble	dbl. tr. or d tr	Triple treble	tr tr
Yarn over hook	yoh or yo or O	Wool round hook	wrh or yrh
Chain	ch		
Decrease	dec	*(English same as American and*	
Increase	inc	*Canadian for the remainder.)*	
Pattern	pat		
Stitch(es)	st		
Beginning	beg		
Slip	sl		
Together	tog		
Remain	rem		
Inches	"		
Round	rnd		
Loop	lp		
Popcorn stitch	pc or pc st		
Space	sp		
Skip	sk		
Picot	p		

CROCHET DEFINITIONS

In crochet, the first row or starting round is worked in a chain.

Row: Term applied to work done back and forth in rows. Here's how you can tell if the next row is a right-side row (even number): If the tail of yarn at the beginning of the foundation chain is on the left side, the right side of the work is facing you and you are working on a right-side or even-numbered row.

196

Row 1: The first row crocheted onto the foundation chain.

Round: Term applied to work done around a center ring or chain. When working in rounds, the right side of the work should always be facing you unless the directions specify otherwise. The right side is facing you as you work the first round.

(. . .): Parentheses mean to repeat the instructions between the parentheses as many times as specified. For example, "(1 sc in next 2 sc. 2 sc in next sc) 4 times" means to do what is in the parentheses 4 times.

Even/Work even: Continue working without increasing or decreasing.

CROCHET HOOKS

The directions at the beginning of each pattern will tell you what size hook and what weight yarn to use. If you tend to crochet tightly, use a larger hook than the instructions call for. If you tend to crochet loosely, use a smaller hook. Crochet a swatch first to gauge your work and then make adjustments in hook size, if necessary.

TYPES OF CROCHET HOOKS:

Steel crochet hooks: Best for cotton thread in small sizes and cotton and wool yarns in large sizes. English sizes range from 00, the largest, to 16, the smallest. American sizes range from 16, the smallest, to 10¼ or K, the largest.

Plastic hooks: Used for wool yarn, man-made fibers and cotton thread. Sizes range from 1, smallest, to 10½, largest. They are also sized according to letters. Q is a giant-size hook.

Aluminum hooks: Used for cotton, wool and man-made fiber yarns. Sizes range from 1 or A, smallest, to 10¼ or K, largest.

Bone hooks: Used for wool yarn. Sizes range from 1, smallest, to 6, largest.

Wooden hooks: Used for rugs with heavy cotton or wool yarns. Sizes range from 10 to 15.

LENGTH OF HOOKS: Crochet hooks vary in length. The average length, used in all projects in this book, is 5½" or 14 centimeters.

CROCHET HOOKS: LARGEST TO SMALLEST

American																				
Letters:		Q	P	K	J	I	H	H	G	F	E	D	C	B	A				
Numbers:				10½/10¼	10	9	8	8	6	5	4	3	2	1	1				
English & Canadian:	000	00	0	2	3	4	5	6	7	8	9	10	11	12	13	14	16		
Metric:	10	9	8	7.50	7	6.50	6	5.50	5	4.50	4	3.50	3.25	3/2.75	2.50	2.25	2	1.75	1.25	1

CROCHET HOOK AND YARN CHART

Yarn Group	Hook Size	Approximate number of single and double stitches per inch
Baby Yarn	C, D, E	7 to 6
Sport Yarn (2 ply)	E, F, G	5½ to 4½
Knitting Worsted (3 to 4 ply)	F, G, H	4½ to 3½
Double Knitting Yarn (close to knitting worsted or use double sport yarn)	G, H	3½ to 3
Bulky Yarn, Craft Yarn (Double knitting worsted)	G, H, I	3¼ to 2½
Rug Yarn, Very Bulky Yarn (1 strand double knitting plus 1 strand bulky)	H, I, J	2¾ to 2
Double Rug Yarn	I, J, K	2¼ to 1¾

• CROCHET INSTRUCTIONS

SLIP KNOT: Pull this piece of yarn through the loop around your fingers.

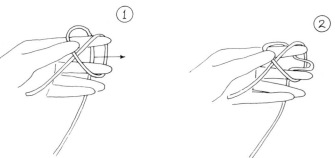

Slide the yarn off your fingers. It will look like illustration 3.

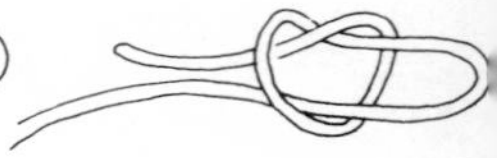

Pull ends tightly.

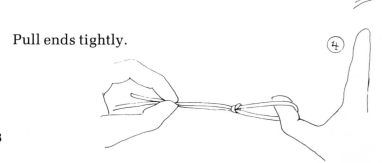

Why is a slip knot called a slip knot? Hold the knot between two fingers and pull the long end. As you pull, the loop "slips" and becomes smaller.

Now slide the loop into a crochet hook and you are ready to crochet.

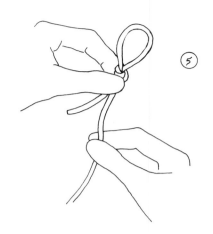

CHAIN OR FOUNDATION CHAIN (ch): With the slip knot on the hook, hold the starting knot between the thumb and first finger of the left hand. Bring the yarn from behind the hook over the hook and to the front. Catch the yarn with the hook and pull it through the loop on the hook. You have made one chain—it should look like illustration 2. Illustration 3 shows a longer chain. Illustration 3a shows an enlargement of the chain.

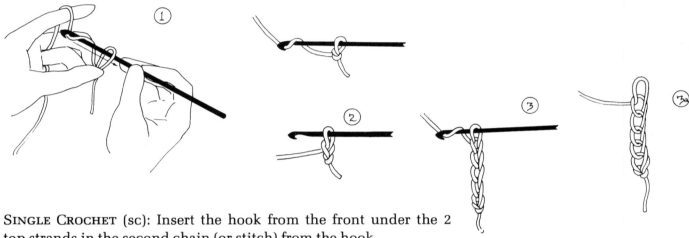

SINGLE CROCHET (sc): Insert the hook from the front under the 2 top strands in the second chain (or stitch) from the hook.

Pass the yarn up and over the hook to the front (yo). Pull the hooked yarn through the chain, making two loops on the hook.

Pass the yarn up and over the hook to the front again (yo). Pull the hooked yarn through both loops, making one new loop on the hook. You have completed one single crochet (sc).

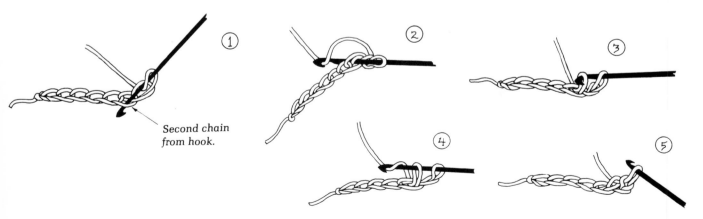

Second chain from hook.

199

Rows of Single Crochet: When you reach the end of a row of single crochet, chain 1.

Turn the work so that the other side is facing you. Insert the hook from the front under the 2 top strands of the first single crochet. Continue on from there. It's not hard to end up with too few or too many stitches in a row, so count your stitches to make sure you have the correct number in each row.

Double Crochet (dc): Chain the number of stitches called for in the instructions.

Pass the yarn from behind over the top of the hook (yo). Insert the hook (with the extra twist of yarn on it) under the 2 top strands of the 4th chain from the hook.

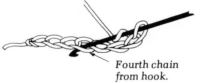

Fourth chain from hook.

Pass the yarn over (yo) the hook again and pull it through the stitch. Now there are three loops on the hook.

Yarn over again. Pull through two loops. There are two loops left on the hook.

Yarn over again. Pull through two loops. One loop is left on the hook, completing one double crochet stitch (dc).

TREBLE (tr): Chain the number of stitches called for in the instructions.

Wrap yarn over hook 2 times. Insert hook under 2 top strands of 5th chain from hook.

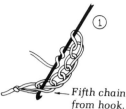

← Fifth chain from hook.

Yarn over hook again and pull it through the stitch. Now there are four loops on hook.

(Yarn over. Pull through two loops) 3 times.

SLIP STITCH (sl st): Chain the number of stitches called for in the instructions.

Insert the hook from the front under the 2 top strands in the second chain from the hook. Yarn over the hook. In one motion, pull the hooked yarn through the loop and through the stitch on the hook. To continue the slip stitch, insert the hook under the 2 top strands of the next chain. Yarn over. Pull all the way through, etc.

SLIP STITCH

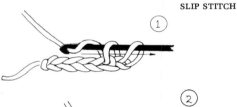

The slip stitch can also be used as a joining stitch. It makes a flat seam. Often it is used to make the ring which is the start of circular crochet projects.

Insert the hook through the 2 top strands of the stitch where the join is to be made. Yarn over.

In one motion, pull the hooked yarn through the loop and the stitch on the hook.

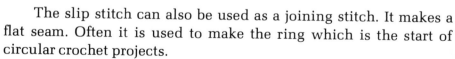

201

DECREASING SINGLE CROCHET: With one stitch already on the hook, pull up a loop through each of the next two stitches. Yarn over. Pull through all three loops on hook. One decrease is complete and there is one less stitch in the row.

DECREASING DOUBLE CROCHET: Work a double crochet to the point where two loops are on the hook. Then work the next double crochet to the same point. There will be four loops on the hook. Yarn over and through two loops. Yarn over and through three loops. One decrease is complete.

DECREASING AT THE END OF A ROW: Just leave the number of stitches to be decreased at the end of the row unworked.

INCREASING (inc): To increase by one stitch, make two stitches in the same opening.

TO INCREASE AT THE END OF A ROW: Make a chain of the required number of stitches at the end of the row. Turn the piece and work those stitches just like the rest.

TURNING THE WORK AT THE END OF A ROW: When you reach the end of a crochet row a certain number of chain stitches are usually done so that the next row will start in the right place. If you are working in single crochet, chain one before turning your work. If you are working in double crochet, chain three before turning. The turning chain counts as the first stitch except in single crochet. There the chain is necessary to make a straight edge and to get you in position to begin the next row.

CHANGING COLORS: To change the color of a new row, start the color change at the end of the old row. Insert hook in last stitch on row. Yarn over. Draw loop through (two loops on hook). Drop the old color. Loop new color around hook and pull that loop through both loops of the old color. If the project is being done in single crochet, chain one before turning your work.

JOINING YARN ENDS:

These ends may be tied together, but it is not necessary.

METHOD 1: Tie yarn ends together in a loose knot. When you have completed the piece, untie the knots and weave the ends through the stitches with a crochet hook so they can't be seen.

METHOD 2: Tie a good knot and crochet over the cut ends of yarn. This method saves time because the ends will be covered as you go.

FINISHING/ENDING OFF: When a piece of work is finished (or where the yarn runs out or is to be cut) cut the yarn about 6″ from the last stitch. Pull the yarn end through the last loop on the hook so that it is tight. Then weave the yarn end into the work so it can't be seen.

BLOCKING: Blocking isn't essential with these animals but it does make the finished project look extra nice. If you want to block, see the blocking instructions in the Knitting section.

SEWING TOGETHER: Edges can be sewn together in several ways. They can be woven together (illustration 1), whipstitched together (2), back stitched together (3), slip stitched together (4), or single crocheted together (5). Single crocheting done on the right side gives a nice ridged effect. The turtle shell is an example.

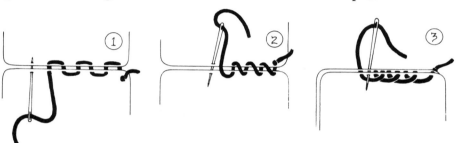

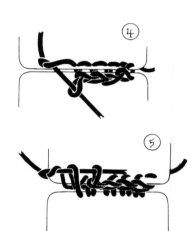

If you are stitching the pieces together, use a large blunt-pointed needle with a large eye (a yarn needle or a tapestry needle). Make stitches loose enough to match the elasticity of your crocheting.

The technique used is determined by the type of join being made. Use whatever stitch is easiest for you unless the directions specify something else.

HOW TO CROCHET LEFT-HANDED

A left-handed person works from left to right while a right-handed person works from right to left. The directions for all the stitches apply to both right-handed and left-handed people. The only difference is that the instructions for a left-handed person are the mirror image of the instructions for a right-handed person.

Note: To use instructions for a right-handed person, if you are left-handed, put a pocket mirror at the left of the illustration. The reflection in the mirror will show you how to work.

GAUGE/TENSION: Although there is no mention of gauge in these patterns, the gauge is often given at the beginning of a pattern. It tells the number of stitches to the inch and sometimes the number of rows to the inch. For example, it might say: "Gauge: 8 rows= 4"." The gauge is a measurement determined by the size of the hook and the weight of the yarn. Gauge is important when you are trying to crochet something to a specific size, like a sweater or a glove. With animal patterns, gauge is not really important. As long as you crochet using about the same tension on your yarn throughout, things will match up close enough. The only thing to worry about is if you tend to crochet much tighter than normal.

CORRECT YARN TENSION: If the stitch is just loose enough to allow the hook to slip through the work easily, your yarn tension is neither too tight nor too loose.

You are crocheting too tightly if your work does not lie flat when it's supposed to. If it doesn't lie flat, try working looser or switch to a larger hook.

LOOSE VS. TIGHT CROCHET: Sometimes when people follow a pattern they feel like they have to crochet tighter than they would ordinarily. There must be a psychological reason for it though I don't know what it is. If you fall into this category, resist the temptation to crochet tighter. Looser stitches work better than tight. Watch out for synthetic yarns though. If you crochet really loosely with them, they tend to stretch out of shape.

AVERAGE GAUGE: With knitting worsted, a #G hook will give you 4 sc per inch.

HOW TO DESIGN YOUR OWN CROCHET PATTERN

Design an animal pattern in muslin or use one from a book or magazine. Draw the outlines of all the pattern pieces on a large sheet of paper. Newspaper and a waterproof marker work well.

Then start crocheting, laying your work down on the drawing regularly to see that it matches the outline of the sketch. Increase and decrease as needed to fit the outline.

Any animal pattern can be crocheted since it is such a versatile technique. Pick up stitches anywhere along the edge of your work to add parts (like legs) where they belong.

It's easier than you can imagine. Try it out on a favorite animal pattern or take the plunge and make your own creation from scratch.

As long as you crochet something close to the shape of the original pattern, it can be stretched a little for perfect matching.

If two or more sides or parts are the same, count stitches and rows from the first piece to get the rest the same.

For even greater accuracy, make a grid as described in "How to Design Your Own Knit Pattern," p. 172.

The Projects

The following seven projects appear in the Knitting section, but you can easily work them in crochet if you prefer. Simply crochet pieces to the measurements indicated below. Crochet ears and other features for the puppets using the illustrations as a guide. To assemble the animals, see the directions and illustrations in the Knitting section.

ELEPHANT (p. 174)
    Body: 8" x 26"
    Ears: 3" x 4½"
    Trunk: 5½" x 3"

OWL (p. 175)
    Body: 8" x 26"
    Face: 4" x 5"
    Wings: 5" x 7"
    Beak: 2" x 2"
    Legs: See knit instructions for crochet directions.

CAT (p. 176)
    Body: 8" x 26"
    Ears: 2½" x 2½"

TURTLE (p. 177)
    Body: 7½" x 16"
    Head: 8" x 4"
    Legs: 4" x 4"

THE ANY-ANIMAL PUPPET (p. 178)
    Body: 8" x 9"

MR. BIG-MOUTH PUPPET (p. 179)
Body: 3½″ x 22″

FINGER PUPPETS (p. 180)
Body: 2½″ x 2½″ average size. (See octopus crochet instructions in the Knitting section.)

• QUICK KIWI

This nutty New Zealander is an easy solution to what to give anybody and everybody. After you've made one, you can easily vary it a hundred ways using different yarns, making longer and shorter beaks, legs and necks. And every one of them is a friend indeed.

MATERIALS
    #I crochet hook
    3 oz. knitting worsted
    2 oz. mohair or mohair combination in same color as knitting worsted (or in a color that goes well with it)
    1 oz. double knitting yarn in a contrasting color (for beak and legs)
    Polyester fiberfill stuffing or nylon net
    Felt scraps, or #G hook, bits of black and white yarn and a yarn needle, for eyes

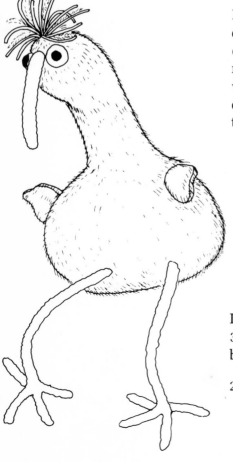

BODY: Crochet the knitting worsted and mohair together. The first couple of rounds will be hard because the mohair fluff makes it difficult to find the holes. But don't worry. As long as you get the right number of stitches in somehow it will look fine. The mohair will also cover minor errors. By the third round it will be much easier so hang on for the beginning. Start at the head. Ch 3. Sl st tog to form ring. 6 sc in ring.
    Rnd 2: 2 sc in each sc. (12 sc.)
    Rnd 3: (1 sc in 1st sc. 2 sc in 2nd sc) around. (18 sc.)
    Rnds 4–20: Sc around. (This finishes the head and neck.)
    Rnds 21–28: (Start of body.) Inc 4 evenly spaced (50 sc.)
    Rnd 29: Inc 2 evenly spaced.
    Rnds 30–32: Sc around.
    Rnd 33: Dec 2 evenly spaced. (50 sc.)
    Rnds 34–39: Dec 4 evenly spaced. (26 sc.)
    Rnds 40–43: Dec 6 evenly spaced. (2 sc.) End off.

LEGS: Make 2, using contrasting color and same crochet hook. Ch 30. Sl st back 6 sc. (Ch 6. Sl st back 5 sc) 3 times to make claws. Sl st back up leg. Tie legs to kiwi.

Note: Make the legs longer if you want. For extra stiffness you could sl st the length of the leg again.

BEAK: Use same color as legs. Ch 12. Sl st the length of the chain 3 times. Tie beak to kiwi's head.

WINGS: Make 2, using body yarns. Ch 6. Dc in 2nd ch from hook and dc across. Ch 2. Turn.

> *Row 2:* Dc across. Ch 2. Turn.
> *Row 3:* Dc in 2 sc. End off and sew to body.

HAIR: Loop yarn through top of head.

EYES: Make eyes out of felt scraps or crochet.

> To crochet eyes, use #G hook and white yarn. Ch 2. 6 sc in 2nd ch from hook. Sl st into next sc to round off and end off. Attach eyes to bird with a large french knot or a few satin stitches in black.

Variation

> Shorten the Kiwi's neck, beak and legs and you've got a chicken.

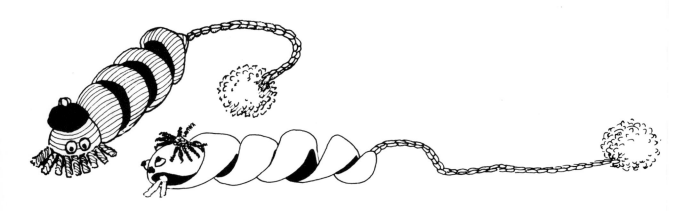

• CORKY, THE BOOKWORM

Corky makes an excellent book marker, tree or plant ornament, decoration for a package or a secret toy to hide in small pockets. It is a very quick project, averaging a half hour.

MATERIALS

> 6½ to 8 yds. knitting worsted. (Variegated yarns look especially nice.)
> #G crochet hook

Bits of yarn and felt for decoration. (The tiny wiggly button eyes sold in sewing shops are very effective.)

Ch 65. Turn. 5 dc in 3rd ch from hook. (3 dc in next ch) 12 times. 2 dc and 1 sc in next ch, drawing yarn through to finish off.

Make a small pompom and attach it to end of tail. Make 2 french knots for eyes or make them out of felt or use wiggly buttons. Tie a piece of yarn to top of head and fluff it out for hair. Or crochet a beanie: Ch 3. Sl st into ring. Sc around for 2 rows. Sc in every other sc in 3rd row and draw yarn through to finish off. Attach to head with french knot.

Make a tongue by knotting a bit of red yarn in his mouth. Or give him whiskers by hooking yarn through the front of his face in a fringe.

The possibilities are endless.

• DRAGONFLY AND BUTTERFLY

Sometimes called the "devil's darning needle," the dragonfly and his butterfly variation are the delicate members of our yarn animal collection. These life-size little creatures would look lovely perched on a barrette or floating between the branches of a Christmas tree.

The patterns given are basic but they offer a special opportunity to more advanced crocheters. If you are one of those gifted people who can crochet beautiful lace doilies, add detailed and special wings of your own design to the basic body. Just think of all the incredible winged creatures you can create!

MATERIALS
    Crochet cotton, carpet warp or dishcloth cotton
    Appropriate crochet hook
    White glue

BODY: Ch 26. Sc in 2nd ch from hook. Sl st the length of the chain. Sl st down other side of chain. Sl st outside edges together. Loop one end of body strip back onto itself and crochet it down to make a head.

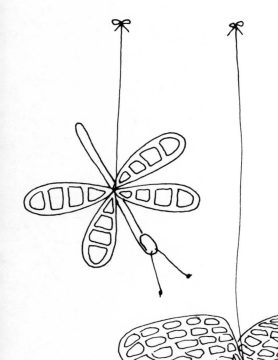

ANTENNAE: Ch 8. Sl st to front of head. Ch 8. End off.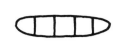

SMALL DRAGONFLY WINGS: (Ch 16. Dc in 8th ch from hook. Ch 1. Dc in 10th ch from hook. Ch 1. Dc in 12th ch from hook. Ch 1. Sl st tog) 4 times to make 4 connected wings. Leave starting and ending threads on wings. Use those threads to tie wings to body about ½" from head.

LARGE DRAGONFLY WINGS OR REAR BUTTERFLY WINGS: Ch 6. 2 tr in 5th ch from hook. 1 tr in last ch.
    Rows 2–3: Ch 3. 1 tr in each tr across. 2 tr in last tr.
    Row 4: Ch 3. 1 tr in each tr across.
    Row 5: Ch 3. Skip 1st tr. 1 tr in each tr across, skipping last tr.
    Row 6: Ch 3. Skip 1st tr. 1 tr in each tr across, skipping last tr.
Ch 3. Sl st to last tr and end off.

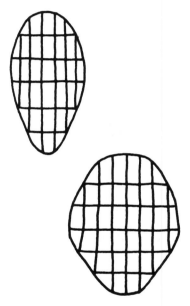

FRONT BUTTERFLY WINGS: Ch 7. 2 tr in 5th ch from hook. 1 tr in next ch. 2 tr in last ch.
    Rows 2–3: Ch 3. 2 tr in 1st tr. Tr across. 2 tr in last tr.
    Row 4: Ch 3. 1 tr in each tr across.
    Row 5: Ch 3. Skip 1st tr. 1 tr in each tr across, skipping last tr.
    Row 6: Ch 3. Skip 1st tr. 1 tr in each tr across, skipping last tr.
Ch 3. Sl st to last tr and end off.

To assemble, sew wings ½" from head, with second set of wings just behind them.

STIFFENING SOLUTION: Mix 1 part white glue and 1 part water. Soak dragonfly and butterfly in solution. Squeeze out excess glue.
    Lay a sheet of wax paper on a piece of corrugated cardboard. Stretch the stiffened wings on the wax paper, holding them in shape with straight pins. Let dry.
    If you want the wings in a flying position rather than flat, dry them first in a flat position. Then moisten them at the point where you want them to bend and prop them in the correct position until they are dry.

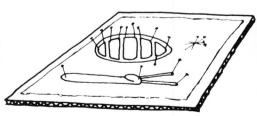

    The dragonflies and butterflies make a beautiful mobile. Consider doing them in colored crochet cotton. To make them extra large, try using cotton yarn.

• PIGGY BAG

Here's a practical gift for a young lady who loves stuffed animals and who needs to carry certain belongings with her wherever she goes.

If you'd like to make a Piggy Pajama Bag, follow the same pattern using doubled rug yarn and a #K hook.

MATERIALS

    6 oz. pink knitting worsted

    Bits of black yarn

    #G hook

BODY: Ch 4. Join with sl st to form ring.

    Rnd 1: 6 sc in ring. Do not join. Mark beg of rnds.

    Rnd 2: 2 sc in each sc. (12 sc.)

    Rnd 3: (1 sc in next sc. 2 sc in next sc) 6 times. (18 sc.)

    Rnds 4–16: Sc around, increasing 4 sc evenly spaced each rnd. Do not work increases over those in previous rows. (70 sc at rnd 16.)

    Rnds 17–32: Work even.

    Rnds 33–39: Sc around, dec 1 each rnd. Sl st tog. Ch 4 at end of rnd 39.

    Rnd 40: Dc in 2nd sc from ch. Ch 2. (Skip a stitch. Dc. Ch 2.) around. Sl st tog. (You've just made holes for drawstring.) Ch 2.

    Rnd 41: 2 dc through first space. (1 sc in next space. 3 dc in next space) around. Sl st tog and end off.

DRAWSTRING: Ch 120. Sl st along chain. End off. Weave chain through holes at top of bag. Make 2 small tassels and tie to both ends of chain.

SNOUT: Work same as body for 3 rnds. (18 sc.)

> *Rnd 4:* Sc around, inc 6 evenly spaced. (24 sc.)
> *Rnd 5:* Sc around, through back loops only.
> *Rnds 6–7:* Sc around. End off.
> Stuff and sew 2½" down from top of bag.

EARS: Make 2, or 4 for extra stiffness. Starting from the tip, ch 2.

> *Row 1:* 3 sc in 2nd ch from hook. Ch 1. Turn.
> *Row 2:* Sc across. Ch 1. Turn.
> *Rows 3–5:* 2 sc in 1st sc. Sc across. 2 sc in last sc. Ch 1. Turn.
> *Row 6:* 2 sc in 1st sc. Sc across. 2 sc in last sc. End off.

Sl st ears tog in pairs for added stiffness. Sew to sides of head, 1½" down from bag opening. Curve upper corner to the front and down a bit. See illustration p. 210.

LEGS: Make 4. Work same as snout for 4 rnds. (24 sc.)

> *Rnds 5–11:* Work even. End off. Add hooves.

HOOVES: With bottom of leg facing you, sl st yarn (either pink or black) through 4th rnd and sc through and around 4th rnd, making a ridge. End off.

> Stuff legs and sew to bottom of bag. See illustration.

TAIL: Ch 10. Starting in 2nd ch from hook, work 2 sc in each ch across. End off and sew to back of pig.

EYES: Make from felt and glue on, or sew on buttons, or crochet black circles and sew on.

• TURTLE WITH REMOVABLE SHELL

(Shown on p. 212.)

Mr. Turtle is a dress-up animal with a removable shell and hat. Although there is nothing more difficult than the popcorn stitch in this project, there are many separate pieces to make and put together. It takes a little patience but the result is extra special. The turtle's shell is buttoned on with popcorn stitches. Add the little hat that Marjorie Frazer designed and you'll have to agree that the turtle is a treasure.

MATERIALS

> 4 oz. knitting worsted in body color (dark green)
> Small amounts of bulky yarn in mixed colors for shell (yellow,

yellow-orange and orange)
#G and #H hooks
Stuffing

HEAD: Using "G" hook and body color, ch 2. Work 6 sc in 2nd ch from hook. Mark beg of rnds.

> *Rnd 2:* 2 sc in each sc. (12 sc.)
> *Rnd 3:* (1 sc in next sc. 2 sc in next sc) 6 times. (18 sc.)
> *Rnds 4–6:* Sc around, inc 4 sc evenly spaced each rnd.
> *Rnd 7:* Sc around. Inc 3 sc evenly spaced. (33 sc.)
> *Rnds 8–13:* Work even.
> *Rnd 14:* (1 sc in next sc. Dec 1 sc.) 11 times. (22 sc.)
> *Rnd 15:* (1 sc in each of next 4 sc. Dec 1 sc) 7 times. (14 sc.) End off.

LEGS: Make 4. Work same as head (in body color) for 3 rnds. (18 sc.)

> *Rnd 4:* (2 sc in next sc. 1 sc in each of next 2 sc) 6 times. (24 sc.)
> *Rnd 5:* Sc around. Dec 6 sc evenly spaced. (18 sc.)
> *Rnds 6–12:* Work even. Fasten off.

BACK: Using body color, work same as legs for 4 rnds. (24 sc.)

> *Rnds 5–10:* Sc around. Inc 8 evenly spaced each rnd, being careful not to inc over inc in previous rnd. (72 sc.)
> *Rnds 11, 13, 15 and 17:* Work even.
> *Rnds 12, 14, 16:* Sc around. Inc 4 evenly spaced. (84 sc.)
> *Rnds 18–19:* Sc around. End off.

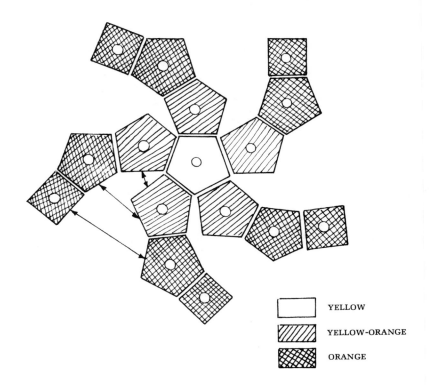

YELLOW

YELLOW-ORANGE

ORANGE

BELLY: Using body color, work same as legs for 4 rnds. (24 sc.)

Rnds 5–14: Sc around. Inc 6 every rnd, being careful not to inc over inc in previous rnd. (84 sc.). End off. Sew to back and stuff. Stuff and sew head and legs to body. See illustrations opposite and p. 214.

TAIL: Using body color, ch 12. Sl st into ring. Sc around.

Rnds 2–3: Dec all around. (*Rnd 2:* 6 sc. *Rnd 3:* 3 sc.)

Rnds 4–5: Work even.

Rnd 6: Dec and end off. Sew to turtle. See illustration.

TURTLE SHELL PATCHES: Using #H hook and bulky yarn make 11 pentagons (1 yellow, 5 yellow-orange and 5 orange) and 5 squares (orange).

PENTAGON: Ch 6. Sl st into ring. Ch 3.

Rnd 2: 2 dc into ring. Ch 3. (3 dc into ring. Ch 3) 4 times. End off.

SQUARE: Ch 6. Sl st into ring. Ch 3.

Rnd 2: 2 dc into ring. Ch 3. (3 dc into ring. Ch 3) 3 times. End off.

To assemble, see illustration p. 214. Safety-pin or sew the shell pieces together, right side out, so that you know everything is matched up. Crochet the pieces together on the outside using the body color. Then sc a border around the bottom of the shell.

TURTLE SHELL BOTTOM: See illustration above. Use #H hook and bulky yarn (yellow or yellow-orange). To start, ch 12. Sl st tog into a ring.

　　Rnd 2: Ch 4. 2 tr into ring. Ch 6. (3 tr. Ch 6) 5 times. Join with sl st.

　　Rnd 3: Ch 2. Sc around. Join with sl st.

　　Rnd 4: (Ch 4. 2 tr. End off with popcorn stitch: Ch 3. 4 dc in the same spot. Drop loop from hook. Insert hook from front to back in top of starting ch 3 and pull dropped loop through. Ch 1 tightly. Cut yarn 6″ from last stitch and tie off.) Tie on yarn at the beginning of the next tr group and follow the instructions between the parentheses until you have completed 6 prongs, each ending with a popcorn stitch.

　　Using the popcorn stitches as buttons, and the holes in the pentagons and squares as buttonholes, button the shell around the turtle's body (see illustration above).

FACE: See illustration p. 212.

EYES: Make 2 in white, using #G hook and knitting worsted. Ch 2. Sc 4 times into 2nd ch from hook. Sl st 1 to join into a ring. Sew to head using a large french knot.

NOSE: Satin stitch a nose to the face in a contrasting color.

214

MOUTH: Sew a large french knot to the face in orange or red.

HAIR: Using body-color yarn or a contrasting color, wrap yarn around 3 fingers 8 times. Tie the yarn tightly in the middle. Clip the loops and tie the hair to the top of the head.

TURTLE'S HAT: Crochet a pentagon, just like the ones for the shell. Single crochet around the pentagon in a contrasting color twice. Then slip stitch around the outside and end off.

Slip stitch underneath, at the edge of the inside pentagon (second row back from edge). Single crochet around the slip stitch. End off.

Make a chain-stitch strap to hold the hat on. Slip stitch back along the chain for extra strength if you want.

Sew a little pompom on top of the hat.

Note: The turtle doesn't have to be green. It looks beautiful with a white body and a shell made of different shades of blue. The only thing to remember if you change the turtle's colors is not to make the turtle shell bottom and the outside row of the turtle shell top the same color. If they are the same, the popcorn stitch buttons won't show up. Another suggestion is to crochet the shell patches together with the same yarn used for the center patch on the shell.

• WALRUS

If you're looking for a BIG return for your time, this Arctic gentleman is it—a large, cuddly toy which works up quickly. The only challenge is to keep count of your rows, and you'll find several easy solutions right below in the Notes.

MATERIALS

    28 oz. bulky yarn or rug yarn in body color (if you want stripes rather than solid, buy an even number of skeins of each color, because you'll be crocheting 2 strands together)
    1 oz. contrasting color rug yarn, if body is in one color
    Small amounts black and white knitting worsted
    #K and #G hooks
    Stuffing—polyester is good

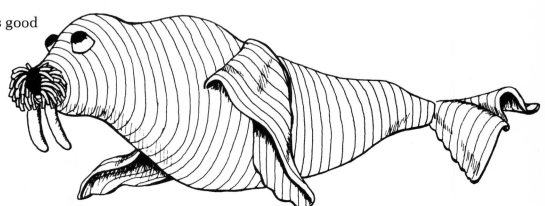

Notes: Although stitch counts are given regularly, the exact count is not essential. A few stitches off here and there will not noticeably change the shape of the walrus.

When you come to the end of a ball of yarn, tie the beginning of the new ball to the end of the old and keep going.

If you mark a specific round with a safety pin or strand of yarn it is easy to keep count. For example, put a marker at Rnd 40 and crochet the next 10 rnds. Then move the marker to Rnd 50, and so on. That way you'll never have to count back more than 10 rnds to know exactly where you are.

BODY: To make the body, crochet 2 strands of yarn tog using #K hook. Work from nose to tail. To begin, ch 2. Sc 5 times in 2nd ch from hook.

Rnd 2: 2 sc in each sc. (10 sc.) Mark beg of rnd.

Odd rnds 3–9: Inc 5 evenly spaced.

Even rnds 4–8: Work even.

Rnd 10: 2 sc in every other sc 4 times. Then sc in each sc to end of rnd. (34 sc.)

Rnds 11–12: Work even.

Rnd 13: (2 sc in next sc. Sc in next sc) 6 times. Then sc in each sc around. (40 sc.)

Rnds 14–15: Sc 20. Then dec to end of rnd. (29 sc.)

Rnd 16: (Sc in next sc. 2 sc in next) 8 times. Then dec every other sc around. (33 sc.)

Rnd 17: (Sc in next sc. 2 sc in next) 10 times. Then dec every other sc around. (37 sc.)

Rnd 18: (Sc in next 3 sc. 2 sc in next) around. (48 sc.)

Rnd 19: Work even.

Rnd 20: (Sc in next 4 sc. 2 sc in next) around. (55 sc.)

Rnds 21–25: Work even.

Rnd 26: Sc 12. Then (2 sc in every other sc) 10 times. Sc 12. Then dec to end of rnd.

Rnd 27: Work 3 dec. Then sc around. (58 sc.)

Rnds 28–36: Work even.

Rnds 37–38: Dec 5 evenly spaced.

Odd rnds 39–47: Work even.

Even rnds 40–48: Dec 5 evenly spaced. (27 sc at rnd 48.)

Rnds 49–55: Work even. Stuff walrus. Crochet the tail end shut at an angle so it looks like the walrus is flipping his tail.

SIDE FLIPPERS: Make 2. Use 2 strands bulky body yarn. To start, ch 21. Sc in 2nd ch from hook and sc across. Ch 1. Turn.

Even rows 2–10: Work even. End off at row 10.

Odd rows 3–9: Sc across. Skip last 2 sc. Ch 1. Turn.

TAIL FLIPPERS: Use 2 strands body yarn. Ch 10. Sc in 2nd ch from hook and sc across. Ch 1. Turn.

Even rows 2–12: Sc across. Skip last 2 sc. Ch 1. Turn. End off at row 12.

Odd rows 3–11: Work even.

TUSKS: Make 2. Use white knitting worsted and #G hook. To begin, ch 2. Sc 4 in 2nd ch from hook.

Rnd 2: Work even.

Rnd 3: (Sc in 1st sc. 2 sc in next) around. (6 sc.)

Rnds 4–5: Work even.

Rnds 6–7: (Sc in 1st sc. 2 sc in next) around. (13 sc.)

Rnds 8–14: To make tusk bend into a curve, crochet 2 sc tog on one side and crochet 2 sc in 1 sc on opposite side, single crocheting between. Always inc and dec at the same place on each rnd.

Rnds 15–16: Work even. End off.

EYES: Use black and white knitting worsted and #G hook. Starting in black, ch 2. Sc 6 in 2nd ch from hook.

Rnd 2: 2 sc in each sc around. (12 sc.)

Rnds 3–5: Change to white. Sc around. End off.

NOSE: Use black knitting worsted and #G hook. Ch 2. Sc 6 in 2nd ch from hook.

Rnds 2–5: (2 sc in 1st sc. Sc in next) around. End off.

To assemble, see illustration p. 215.

Variation

SEAL: Make whiskers same color as body. Leave off tusks. Sew a big pompom ball to end of nose.

• BROOMSTICK DRAGON

Dana was just one year old when she met the broomstick dragon. Without waiting for an introduction she walked over to him, grabbed his neck, threw one leg over the broomstick and rode away.

There are several parts to make but most are done in double crochet so they work up quickly.

MATERIALS

    8 oz. bulky yarn (rug yarn is okay) in green or whatever main color you choose.

    4 oz. bulky red yarn

    2 oz. gold double knitting yarn or knitting worsted

    Small amounts black and white knitting worsted

    Small amount bulky black yarn (or use doubled knitting worsted)

    #K and #G crochet hooks

    Polyfill stuffing

    Broomstick or mop handle

    Furniture tacks, approximately 6

    Fabric scrap, 3″ x 6″

MAIN HEAD PIECE: Make 2. Use main color. Starting from top of head, ch 14. Turn.

Row 1: Dc in 2nd ch from hook. 1 dc in each ch across. 2 dc in last ch. Ch 2. Turn. (15 dc.) (Should be about 6″ long.)

Row 2: Dc across. Ch 2. Turn.

Rows 3, 5, 7: Inc 1 dc.

Rows 4, 6, 8–12: Work even.

Row 13: Dc 17. Ch 12 (to start lower jaw). Turn.

Row 14: Dc in 2nd ch from hook and each ch; continue to dc to back of head. (28 dc.)

Rows 15–17: Work even and end off. (Lower jaw finished.)

INSET: Start at bottom of front edge of jaw. Measure this strip against the main head piece as you go to make sure the colors coincide. Change the pattern wherever necessary to make the colors match.

Using main color, ch 3. Turn. Dc in 2 chains. Ch 2. Turn. Dc across, inc 1 each row for 2 rows. (5 dc.) Work next row even.

Change to red yarn for mouth. Work even for 8″ (approx.).

Change to bulky or doubled black knitting worsted for snout. Work even 3½″ (approx.).

Change to red for spine. Work 21″ (approx.), dec 1 each row for last 2 rows. End off.

SPINE: Work in bulky red. Make a chain 22″ long.

Row 1: Dc in each ch. Ch 2. Turn.

Row 2: Dc in 1st dc. (Dc and ch 4 and dc in same space. Sc in next dc. Sl st in next. Sc in next) repeating to end of chain. End off. Sew spine to middle of inset, starting where the red joins the black at the top of the snout.

TONGUE: Work in bulky red. Ch 7. Turn. Dc in 2nd ch and in each ch across. (6 dc.) Ch 2. Work 3 rows even.

Split for fork in tongue: 2 dc in 1st dc. 1 dc in next dc. Ch 2. Turn. Work 3 rows even. Ch 2. Skip 1 dc. Dc. End off, leaving a 3″ tail of yarn at tip of tongue for "flame."

Pick up on other side of tongue and work to correspond.

EYES: Make 2. Work in knitting worsted using #G hook. Starting with black, ch 2. Sc 6 in 2nd ch from hook.

Rnd 2: 2 sc in each sc around. (12 sc.)

Rnds 3–6: Change to white. Sc around. End off.

NOSTRILS: Make 2. Work in bulky red and bulky or doubled black. Using #K hook, start with red. Ch 2. 6 dc in 2nd ch from hook.

Change to black. Work 3 rnds even in dc. End off.

HORNS: Make 2. Use gold and #G hook. Ch 2. 6 sc in 2nd ch from hook.

Rnd 2: 2 sc in each sc around. (12 sc.)

Rnd 3: (Sc in 1st sc. 2 sc in 2nd sc) around. (18 sc.)

Rnd 4: Inc 4 evenly spaced. (22 sc.)

Rnd 5: Dec all around. (11 sc.)

Rnds 6–12: Work even. End off.

EARS: Make 2. Work in bulky or doubled black. Using #K hook, ch 10. Turn. Dc in 2nd ch from hook and dc across. Ch 2. Turn.

Row 2: Dc across. Ch 2. Turn.

Rows 3–4: Skip 1st dc. Dc across. Ch 2. Turn.

Row 5: Skip 1st dc. Dec 2 dc and end off.

TEETH: After the head is put together you might crochet some teeth around the mouth if you're feeling energetic. Picot stitch would work. Tie on white yarn at back corner of mouth. Work 1 sl st. (Ch 3 to 6, depending on size tooth desired, sl st in top of sl st just made, sl st in next 4 st) all around mouth until you get back to where you started. End off.

To assemble; see illustrations p. 78 in Rya section. Cut fabric strip in half to make two 3″ squares and sew pieces securely to center bottom edge of neck. Fold mouth section of inset in half and sew tongue in the fold. Sew head pieces to inset, carefully matching colors. Leave an 8″ opening on one side of top of head. Slide head, inside out, about 10″ down broomstick handle. Tack fabric strips to broomstick so they will be inside head when head is turned right side out. Turn head right side out. Sew nostrils in place, hooking pieces of red yarn in center to make "flames" coming out. Stuff eyes and horns and sew in place. Sew on ears. Stuff head around broomstick. A good way to pad end of broomstick is to put the end into a partially stuffed sock. Stuff the rest of the sock and tie around stick. Finish stuffing head around sock. Sew shut. Add a rope or heavy cord bridle if you want.

• CROCHETED CAMEL

The only challenge to making this one-humped domesticated dromedary is to follow the instructions. There's lots of increasing and decreasing that doesn't look like it makes sense until you put the animal together. The result is a gangly, awkward, floppy, funny beast.

You might want to use some wire or pipe cleaners to brace his neck. He's a guaranteed winner on any gift list.

MATERIALS
>   #G crochet hook
>   8 oz. gold double knitting yarn
>   4 oz. yellow double knitting yarn
>   Scraps of felt for face
>   Bits of orange yarn (optional)
>   Polyfill stuffing

BODY: Make 2. Start in gold. Ch 17.

Row 1: Sc in 3rd ch from hook. Sc across. (16 sc.) Ch 2. Turn.

Rows 2–3: Inc 2 at beg row. Sc across until 3 sc remain. Inc 1 in each of next 2 sc. Sc in last sc. (24 sc.)

Rows 4–7: Inc 1 in 1st sc. Sc across. Inc 1 in last sc. Ch 2. Turn. (32 sc.)

Rows 8–10: Sc across. Ch 2. Turn.

Row 11: Sc across. Inc 1 in last sc. Ch 2. Turn.

Row 12: Inc 1 at beg of row. Sc across. Ch 2. Turn.

Row 13: Same as 11.

Row 14: Same as 12. (36 sc.)

Row 15: Sc across. Inc 2 at end of row. Ch 2. Turn.

Row 16: Inc 2 at beg of row. Sc across. Ch 2. Turn.

Row 17: Same as 15. (42 sc.)

Row 18: Sc across. Ch 2. Turn.

Row 19: Dec 1 at beg of row. Sc across. Ch 2. Turn.

Row 20: Inc 1 at beg of row. Sc across. Ch 2. Turn.

Row 21: Dec 1 at beg of row. Sc across. (41 sc.) Ch 2. Turn.

Row 22: Sc across. Ch 2.

HUMP:

Row 1 (which is Row 23): Dec 1 at beg of row. Sc 21 across. Ch
2. Turn.

Row 2: Dec 1 at beg of row. Sc across. Ch 2. Turn.

Rows 3–5: Sc across. Ch 2. Turn.

Rows 6–7: Dec 1 at beg of row. Sc across. Ch 2. Turn. (18 sc.)

Row 8: Same as 3.

Rows 9–10: Same as 6.

Change to yellow.

    Rows 11–13: Sc across. Ch 2. Turn.

    Rows 14–16: Dec 1 at beg and end of rows. End off.

NECK: Work in gold. Start at row where hump was joined. Sl st yarn into 8th sc from the hump. Sc in same sc. Sc across. Inc 1 in last sc. Ch 2. Turn. (13 sc.)

    Row 2: Dec 1 at end of row. Ch 2. Turn.

    Row 3: Dec 1 at beg of row and inc 1 at end of row. Ch 2. Turn.

    Row 4: Dec 1 at end of row. Ch 2. Turn.

    Row 5: Dec 1 at beg of row. Sc across. (10 sc.) Ch 2. Turn.

    Rows 6–16: Sc across. Ch 2. Turn.

HEAD:

    Row 17: Inc 2 at end of row. Ch 2. Turn.

    Row 18: Dec 1 at beg of row. Sc across. Ch 2. Turn.

    Row 19: Dec 1 at end of row. (10 sc.) Ch 2. Turn.

    Rows 20–26: Sc across. Ch 2. Turn.

    Row 27: Inc 1 at end of row. Ch 2. Turn.

    Row 28: Inc 1 at beg of row. (12 sc.) Sc across. Ch 2. Turn.

    Row 29: Dec 1 at beg of row. Sc in next 8 sc. Ch 2. Turn. (9 sc.)

    Row 30: Dec 1 at end of row. Ch 2. Turn.

    Row 31: Sc across. End off.

NOSE: Make 2 in yellow. Ch 5.

    Row 1: Sc across. (4 sc.) Ch 2. Turn.

    Row 2: Sc across. Inc 1 sc at end of row. Ch 2. Turn.

    Row 3: Inc 1 sc at beg of row. Sc across. Ch 2. Turn.

    Row 4: Inc 2 at beg of row. Sc across. (8 sc.) Ch 2. Turn.

    Rows 5–9: Sc across. Ch 2. Turn.

    Rows 10–11: Dec 1 at beg and end of rows. Ch 2. Turn. End off.

EARS: Make 4, 2 in gold and 2 in yellow. (Or just make 2 in gold.) Ch 4.

    Row 1: Sc across. (3 sc.) Ch 2. Turn.

    Row 2: 2 sc in each sc across. (6 sc.) Ch 2. Turn.

    Row 3: Inc 1 at beg and end of row. Ch 2. Turn.

    Rows 4–5: Sc across. Ch 2. Turn.

    Row 6: Dec 1 at beg and end of row. Ch 2. Turn.

    Row 7: Dec across. (3 sc.) Ch 2. Turn.

    Row 8: Sc across. End off.

LEGS: Make 4. Start in yellow. Ch 3. Sl st tog. Ch 3.

    Rnd 1: 9 dc in center ring.

    Rnd 2: 2 dc in each dc around. (20 dc.)

    Rnd 3: Work even.

    Rnd 4: Dec 10. (End of foot.)

Rnds 5–10: Work even. *Change to gold to begin knee.*
Rnd 11: (Inc 1 dc in 1st 2 dc and dc in 3rd dc) around.
Rnd 12: Work even.
Rnd 13: (Dec 1 dc in 1st 2 dc. Dc in next dc) around.
Rnds 14–17: Work even. End off.

TAIL: Work in gold. Ch 4. Sl st tog. Ch 2.
Rnd 1: (2 dc in each ch) around. (8 dc.)
Rnds 2–9: Dc around. End off. Tie an orange tassel on end of tail.

To assemble, sew nose pieces to shaped part of head pieces. Sew both body pieces together, leaving an opening at the bottom. Stuff firmly and sew shut. Match yellow ear pieces (if used) with gold. Sew them together and then sew ears to head. Stuff legs and sew them under body. Put a little stuffing in the tail and sew to body.

FRINGE

Using a crochet hook and short lengths of yellow yarn (or orange if you want a nice contrast), fold lengths in half, hook them through where you want the fringe, making a loop, and pull the ends through the loop.

Hook fringe around the ears, around the hump at the line where the colors change, at the end of the tail and under the camel's neck.

Variation

BACTRIAN CAMEL

The Bactrian camel has 2 humps. Follow the pattern except for the section on the hump.

HUMP #1

Row 1 (which is Row 23): Sc 11. Ch 2. Turn.
Row 2: Dec 1 at beg row. Sc across. Ch 2. Turn.
Row 3: Work even.
Row 4: Dec 1 at beg row. Sc across. Ch 2. Turn.
Row 5: Same as Row 4.
Rows 6–7: Work even.
Rows 8–9: Sc across. Dec 1 at end. Ch 2. Turn.
Change to yellow.
Rows 10–12: Work even.
Row 13: Dec 1 at beg of row. End off.
HUMP #2
Tie on gold yarn at stitch next to rear hump (which is 23 again) and work same as Hump #1.

• MEASURES
(approximate equivalents in order of size)

LENGTHS
Centimeter: a little less than ½ inch (0.39 in.)
Inch: 2½ centimeters (2.54 cm.)
Foot: a little less than ⅓ meter (0.3 m.)
Yard: a little less than a meter (0.9 m.)
Meter: a yard plus 3 inches (3.28 ft.)
3 meters: Just under 10 ft.

CONVERSION FROM CENTIMETERS TO INCHES
(based on 1 cm. — .3937in.)

cm.	in.	cm.	in.	cm.	in.	cm.	in.
1	½	27	10¾	53	20¾	79	31
2	¾	28	11	54	21¼	80	31½
3	1¼	29	11½	55	21¾	81	32
4	1½	30	11¾	56	22	82	32¼
5	2	31	12¼	57	22½	83	32¾
6	2¼	32	12½	58	22¾	84	33
7	2¾	33	13	59	23¼	85	33½
8	3¼	34	13½	60	23½	86	33¾
9	3½	35	13¾	61	24	87	34¼
10	4	36	14¼	62	24½	88	34¾
11	4¼	37	14½	63	24¾	89	35
12	4¾	38	15	64	25¼	90	35½
13	5	39	15¼	65	25½	91	35¾
14	5½	40	15¾	66	26	92	36¼
15	6	41	16¼	67	26½	93	36½
16	6¼	42	16½	68	26¾	94	37
17	6¾	43	17	69	27¼	95	37½
18	7	44	17¼	70	27½	96	37¾
19	7½	45	17¾	71	28	97	38¼
20	7¾	46	18	72	28¼	98	38½
21	8¼	47	18½	73	28¾	99	39
22	8¾	48	19	74	29¼	100	39½
23	9	49	19¼	75	29½	101	39¾
24	9½	50	19¾	76	30	102	40¼
25	9¾	51	20	77	30¼	103	40½
26	10¼	52	20½	78	30¾	104	41

WEIGHTS
Gram: 0.035 oz. (very light)
20 grams: less than ¾ oz.
25 grams: ⅞ oz.
Ounce: 28.3 gr.
40 grams: 1⅖ oz.
50 grams: 1¾ oz.
100 grams: 3½ oz.
Pound: 453.6 gr. or approx ½ kilogram (.4536 k)
Kilogram: a little over 2 pounds (2.2 lb.)

If the yarn you want is sold in grams instead of ounces here is an *Easy Conversion Chart*

Oz. ball		50 gr. ball		40 gr. ball		25 gr. ball		20 gr. ball
1	use	1	or	1	or	2	or	2
2		2		2		3		3
3		2		2		4		5
4		3		3		5		6
8		5		6		9		12
16		9		11		19		23